HEALING
HEALTHCARE

A Study and Action Guide
on Healthcare Access
in the United States

Edited by Joseph J. Kotva Jr.

Essays by Karl S. Shelly
Willard M. Swartley
John D. Roth
Phyllis J. Miller
Timothy Stoltzfus Jost
Joseph J. Kotva Jr.

Teacher Guide by Dale Shenk

Faith & Life
Resources

a division of Mennonite
Publishing Network

Anabaptist Center
for Healthcare Ethics

Healing Healthcare: A Study and Action Guide on Healthcare Access in the United States

Edited by Joseph J. Kotva Jr.

Copyright © 2005 by Faith & Life Resources, a division of Mennonite Publishing Network, Scottdale, Pa. 15683

International Standard Book Number: 0-8361-9310-5

Design by Kevin Cook

Printed in the United States of America

This study guide is a cooperative effort of the Healthcare Access Commission of Mennonite Church USA (which funded editorial costs), the Anabaptist Center for Healthcare Ethics, and Faith & Life Resources.

Contents

Read essays, especially 6 — what is unique contributions Mennos need to make

Introduction

Welcome to *Healing Healthcare: A Study and Action Guide on Healthcare Access in the United States.* You are to be commended for engaging the issue of healthcare access. Healthcare, or lack thereof, touches nearly everyone, including our sisters and brothers in the pews and our neighbors down the street. Given this near omnipresence, Christian love compels us to become better informed about the critical problems facing the U.S. healthcare system and to search for how we as Anabaptist communities can help address those problems. Drawing on experts in healthcare access, this guide works with a learning model that helps you and your group to be better informed, but also to work toward concrete, practical responses.

This study is occasioned by developments in Mennonite Church USA. Recognizing that the U.S. healthcare is facing enormous problems of access and runaway costs, Mennonite Church USA delegates to Atlanta 2003 approved the Healthcare Access Initiative. In 2004, the Mennonite Church USA Executive Board officially appointed a 19-member Healthcare Access Commission to oversee that initiative. Funding this study is among the Healthcare Access Commission's current efforts.

I am grateful to the Commission for encouraging the Anabaptist Center for Healthcare Ethics (ACHE) to take on this project and for their generous funding of it. I am even more grateful to the other contributing authors: Karl S. Shelly, Willard Swartley, John D. Roth, Phyllis J. Miller, Timothy Stoltzfus Jost, and Dale Shenk (see biographical sketches on page 61). Operating within a short production schedule, each author produced rich material that shows forth his or her expertise, experience, and commitment to the church.

We at ACHE would benefit from knowing how study groups are using this guide, and what results are emerging from their engagement with the issues of healthcare access. When you have finished this study, therefore, please feel free to pass your experience on to us at jkotva@ambs.edu or at: ACHE at AMBS, 3003 Benham Ave., Elkhart, IN 46517-1999.

Joseph J. Kotva Jr., Director

Anabaptist Center for Healthcare Ethics

March 2005

Lesson 1
The Current Situation

by Karl S. Shelly

The United States at its best has as good medical care as you'll get anywhere in the world. It really is superb.
—Herbert Pardes, MD, President and CEO of New York Presbyterian Healthcare Network (2000)

The United States has a disintegrating, profit-ridden healthcare non-system. … The stories of real people confronting their healthcare problems show how cruel our system has become. —Dr. John P. Geyman, Professor Emeritus of Family Medicine, University of Washington (2002)

Is our healthcare system "superb" or "cruel"? Does it "bind up the injured, and … strengthen the weak" (Ezekiel 34:16), promote "life abundant" (John 10: 10), and serve the "least of these" (Matthew 25: 40)? Your answer may depend on your personal experiences with the system, as well as the state of your health and financial resources.

Most industry observers agree that runaway costs and millions of uninsured Americans are significant problems with the U.S. healthcare system. Yet no national consensus exists on how to improve the system. This impasse stems in part from the system's complexity and size. Currently, healthcare spending constitutes over 15.3 percent of our country's gross national product ($1.7 trillion in 2003) and is projected to reach 18.7 percent by 2014. In a system this large, many groups and institutions seek to protect their self-interests. One result of such self-protection is that myths are propagated about what does and does not work. Nevertheless, we can begin to get a sense of the health of our national system by asking five basic questions:

1. How do people access healthcare in the United States?

Most Americans—82 percent—have health insurance of some sort. The elderly have Medicare (a federal government health insurance program), and nearly two-thirds of Americans under the age of 65 are insured through their own or a family member's employer. Employer-sponsored insurance has been predominant in the U.S. since

World War II, and is subsidized by the federal government through an employer tax exclusion for health insurance premiums.

There is no requirement that employers offer their workers health benefits, and due to rapidly rising healthcare costs (premiums rose nearly 14 percent from 2002 to 2003), employment-based insurance is declining. Since 2000, the number of Americans with employer-sponsored coverage consistently decreased. In 2003, for example, only 39 percent of those working in companies with less than ten employees received any health benefits through their job.

2. Who are the people without health insurance?

The latest census tells us that over 45 million Americans—more than one in six of the nonelderly population—are uninsured. This number has grown by over 1 million in each of the past four years.

The uninsured are usually not the poorest of the poor, many of whom are eligible for Medicaid. Rather, four out of five (81 percent) of the uninsured are in working families. The uninsured are most often employed in small businesses, service industries, and blue collar jobs. Two-thirds of the uninsured belong to households with income under $50,000.

In contrast to the U.S. population as a whole, the uninsured are younger, poorer, less educated, and more likely to be Latino or African-American. In 2003,

33 percent of Hispanics and 20 percent of African-Americans were uninsured for the entire year.

3. Don't Medicaid and hospital emergency rooms provide an adequate healthcare safety net?

Medicaid was designed to provide low income Americans with health insurance and currently does so for 38 million children and parents. However, Census Bureau data shows that approximately 81 percent of low income adults—people with income below 200 percent of the federal poverty line, currently less than $37,000 for a family of four and less than $18,000 for a single person—do not meet state eligibility requirements and are left uninsured. States have wide latitude in setting eligibility requirements for their residents. As a result, most states provide no coverage for impoverished non-parent adults and only accept parents with extremely low incomes.

Even those eligible for Medicaid have trouble accessing healthcare. Many healthcare providers will not accept Medicaid, especially for dental services. Moreover, all Medicaid recipients regularly risk losing benefits or coverage when state fiscal crises result in healthcare spending cutbacks.

Hospital emergency rooms are required by law to treat all who seek their help, regardless of ability to pay. However, this is an extraordinarily expensive and inefficient way to provide primary care, and it results in little or no continuity of care. Additionally, hospitals often charge uninsured people higher prices than they charge those with coverage, since there is no insurance company to negotiate a discount for them. When faced with a possible two to four hour wait and a $500 bill, it is unsurprising that the uninsured use emergency rooms less frequently overall than do those with insurance and are almost twice as likely as the insured to delay getting needed medical care.

4. What are the consequences of being uninsured?

For thousands of people, the consequence of being uninsured is death. A recent Institute of Medicine study (*Care without Coverage: Too Little, Too Late*, May 2002) estimates that lack of coverage accounts for approximately 18,000 premature deaths annually among uninsured adults under age 65. For example, cancer patients without insurance die sooner, on average, than do otherwise comparable peers with insurance, largely because of delayed diagnosis.

For many others, being uninsured means having poorer health and no regular source of care. In its report, "Sicker and Poorer: The Consequences of Being Uninsured" (February 2003), the Kaiser Commission on Medicaid and the Uninsured documented that "the uninsured receive less preventive care, are diagnosed at more advanced disease stages, and once diagnosed, tend to receive less therapeutic care (drugs and surgical interventions)" (executive summary, 1).

5. How does the U.S. healthcare system compare internationally?

In most economically developed countries, governments guarantee health coverage for their citizens. The U.S. is unique in offering no such guarantee and in that its healthcare system is largely market driven. As a result, state-of-the-art medicine and the latest technology are readily available only to those able to pay and those with adequate insurance.

Further, despite spending significantly more per capita on healthcare than any other country, the United States consistently places outside the top 20 in criteria such as life expectancy, infant mortality, and immunization rates. Also, in a recent comparison with Great Britain, Australia, Canada, and New Zealand, the U.S. scored worst in economic barriers to care, patients' out-of-pocket expenses for needed care, and pain control in emergency rooms.

These healthcare outcomes are in part a product of our market-based, for-profit approach. Aspects of medicine that are highly profitable—diagnostic technology, prescription drugs, high-tech treatment—are superb in the United States, but those that do not generate significant revenue—prevention, education, access to basic care—are given short shrift. This market-based, for-profit approach at least partially accounts for our being inundated with pharmaceutical commercials for various types of erectile dysfunction pills (a decidedly non-fatal condition that is highly lucrative for drug companies) while we simultaneously have a shortage of flu vaccine and 45 million uninsured people. Perhaps the market, which works well to sell cheeseburgers and toothpaste, is poorly equipped to keep a nation healthy and well cared for.

A real life story

Dr. Michelle Schirch Shelly is a Mennonite and a family physician whose practice includes insured and uninsured patients. A few years ago, an insured, single mother of two young children came to Dr. Shelly complaining of abdominal pain. Dr. Shelly discovered a large mass in the patient's uterus which tested positive for a malignancy. The patient was referred to an oncologist who began treatment, but the illness soon prevented the woman from working. Unable to work, her employer fired her, and with her job went her health insurance. Even if she had the money to purchase an individual insurance policy, no insurance company would accept her with a diagnosis of cancer.

Seriously ill, impoverished, and now without health insurance, the woman moved with her young children into her sister's home and applied for Medicaid—that is, government insurance for the poor. To make matters worse, her specialist no longer wanted to treat her because Medicaid paid him lower reimbursement rates than private insurance. It wasn't long before Dr. Shelly started seeing this woman's son for behavioral problems and began treating her sister for anxiety and depression.

The Gospel of Mark also tells of a nameless woman who suffered 12 years from a serious illness. Mark 5:26 says, "She had endured much under many physicians, and had spent all that she had; and she was no better, but rather grew worse." This verse aptly describes the plight of this patient and millions of others who experience the callous side of the U.S. healthcare system. Too often, the uninsured cannot get needed or continuous medical care and are frequently pushed into bankruptcy when a medical emergency arises (according to Consumers Union, February 25, 2004, unreimbursed healthcare costs contribute to half of all personal bankruptcies filed in the U.S.). Such folks endure much and oftentimes do not get better but rather grow worse.

In Mark's gospel, the suffering, impoverished woman without a name reaches out to Jesus. Upon noticing her touch, Jesus delays his trip to the house of Jairus, a well-respected synagogue leader, and gives priority to her, whom he calls "daughter."

What would our healthcare system look like if we saw the millions of uninsured as our "daughters" and "sons"? What priorities would be primary in such a system? Working to find answers to such questions may help bring "good news" to our country and its healthcare system.

To further explore the state of the U.S. healthcare system, see the following nonpartisan resources:

Alliance for Health Reform: www.allhealth.org

The Commonwealth Fund: www.cmwf.org

The Henry J. Kaiser Family Foundation: www.kff.org

Faith Community statements on U.S. healthcare: www.uhcan.org/faith/faith_statements/intro.html

Cover the Uninsured: www.covertheuninsuredweek.org

Lesson 2
The Bible and Christian Convictions

by Willard M. Swartley

What are our basic biblical and Christian convictions about healthcare? Do all people have the right to healthcare access? When we address this issue as Anabaptist Christians, should we advocate "rights" language or basic biblical and Christian moral teachings? I contend that the Christian passion for issues of healthcare access are less rooted in seeking our "rights" than in a missional concern for others.

Jesus taught his disciples to love all people, including their enemies, not because they belong to our group, believe as we do, or choose the good instead of evil. Rather, because the heavenly Father gives rain and sun to the good and evil alike, so we should love all people, even our enemies (Matthew 5:43-48; Luke 6:27-36). Such care for others certainly includes seeking to make healthcare accessible for all.

Five biblical themes and early Christian practices underline the urgency of improving healthcare access for all:

1. Scripture identifies shalom as God's will and gift for people.

Shalom, the Hebrew word for *peace* (210 occurrences; over 350 uses, including derivatives) has many dimensions of meaning: wholeness, well-being, peace, salvation, and justice. Shalom occurs often in inquiring about one's *welfare* (Genesis 26:6; 37:14; 43:27; Exodus 18:7; 1 Samuel 10:4; 17: 18, 22; 25:5; 30:21; Jeremiah 15:5 for shalom of Jerusalem; 38:4). This inquiry about one's "welfare includes everything necessary to healthful living: good health, a sense of well-being, good fortune, the cohesiveness of the community, relationship to relatives and their state of being, and anything else deemed necessary for everything to be in order" (Claus Westermann, "Peace [*Shalom*] in the Old Testament" in *The Meaning of Peace,* ed. Perry B. Yoder and Willard M. Swartley [Elkhart, Ind.: IMS,

2001], 49). English versions may translate shalom as prosperity (Psalm 30:6; Isaiah 54:13). Shalom also has moral connotations: it is opposed to deceit (Psalm 34:13-14; Jeremiah 8:22–9:6). The notion of *well-being* shades over into shalom's cognate, *shalem* (used 33 times), which denotes holistic health.

Shalom assumes relationship with God and meaningful relationships with fellow-humans. Cheating others, hurting others in any way, violating covenants, and living selfishly deprive the community of shalom. When certain people are disqualified from healthcare benefits, they are excluded from experiencing shalom. When a healthcare system excludes the weakest and most vulnerable citizens from basic, non-emergency healthcare coverage it deprives the people excluded of fullness of shalom. Such exclusion obstructs God's moral shalom purpose for humans.

2. Old Testament Scripture emphasizes justice.

Justice describes God's moral nature (Psalm 89:14), and justice often occurs in parallel to righteousness (Psalm 72:1-2; Proverbs 2:9; 8:20; Isaiah 5:7b; 32: 16; 33:5-6; 54:13-14; 60:17b) and shalom/peace (Isaiah 32:16-17; 59:8; cf. Psalm 85:10b; Isaiah 60: 17). But the meaning of justice (*mishpat*) in Hebrew thought is not the same as the Greek view, popular in western society, that each person receives *equal* due. But in the biblical understanding of justice, the needs of the poor, widows, and orphans must be met (Psalm 72:4, 12-14; 146:6b-9).

Assisting the needy is linked often to "the fear of the Lord" (Deuteronomy 10:10-20; cf. Leviticus 25: 17; 35-43; 19:14, 32; Isaiah 33:5-6). Pursuit of this radical justice in communal life was a condition for living in the land God promised to the covenant people: "Justice, and only justice, you shall pursue, so that you may live and occupy the land that the Lord your God is giving you" (Deuteronomy 16:20).

Hear Amos, "Let justice roll down like waters, and righteousness like an ever-flowing stream" (5:24).

The prophets ranted and raved because Israel failed to practice God's justice. Read the following texts and ponder their significance for healthcare access: Isaiah 8:5-10; Amos 8:4-10; Micah 6:1-8; and Nehemiah 5:1-13. These texts indicate that nothing stirs God's wrath against his people more than failure to practice justice by caring for the needy. The same moral priority continues in the New Testament. James says, "Religion that is pure and undefiled before God, the Father, is this: to care for the orphans and widows in their distress, and to keep oneself unstained by the world" (1:27).

3. Jesus modeled healthcare inclusion of the poor and marginalized.

Jesus's healing ministry had an unusual access policy. Most people Jesus healed from illness or delivered from demons were not persons with standing in the religious community or people of means. Jairus' daughter was an exception, since Jairus was a ruler of the synagogue. Approximately a third of those Jesus healed were women. Some were ritually defiled, unclean. Another third were socially ostracized, lepers, Gentiles, and "sinners." There were no exclusions in Jesus's healing ministry. Nor were there exclusions in what Jesus taught about caring for the sick. For example, Jesus says he will separate the sheep from the goats in the judgment of the nations. The sheep (nations?) are those who cared for the hungry, thirsty, naked, and the *sick* (Matthew 25:31-40).

When we consider Jesus's teaching and the social, economic, and political profile of the people he healed, we must conclude that exclusionary policies in healthcare are wrong. As Christians, we cannot morally accept the present U.S. distribution pattern of healthcare services. Indeed, Christian witness to national government on healthcare policy can testify to Jesus's Lordship and can be part of the manifold witness to the powers that Paul speaks about in Ephesians 3:9-10.

4. Sharing material resources was a basic teaching and practice of the New Testament church.

After Pentecost the early church had all things in common (Acts 2:42-45; 4:32-37). Another model of sharing, more applicable to us now, involved collecting money from wealthier Jewish-Gentile Christian churches throughout Asia Minor and Macedonia for the poorer Jewish Christians in Jerusalem. Paul speaks of this relief gift extensively (2 Corinthians 8–9), grounding it in "the grace given me by God" (Romans 15:15). Paul likewise prays that this "offering of the Gentiles may be acceptable, sanctified by the Holy Spirit" (15:16).

Paul describes his relief work at length: "At present, however, I am going to Jerusalem in a ministry (*diakonia*) to the saints; for Macedonia and Achaia have been pleased to share their resources with the poor among the saints at Jerusalem. They were pleased to do this, and indeed they owe it to them; for if the Gentiles have come to share in their spiritual blessings, they ought also to be of service to them in material things" (Romans 15:25-27). Because the assistance was *mutual*, it would be returned if the situation was reversed (2 Corinthians 8:13-15). Such mutual care manifested God's gift of grace in the community. It bonded formerly alienated people into one in Jesus Christ, their peace (Ephesians 2:13-17).

Paul gave his life to practice mutual aid, despite prophesy that he would encounter arrest and imprisonment in Jerusalem (Acts 21:7-14). Paul says, "… I am ready not only to be bound but even to die in Jerusalem for the name of the Lord Jesus Christ" (v. 13b). Paul regarded his relief gift to Jerusalem as the crowning achievement of his apostolic calling since it proved the unity of the Gentiles and the Jews in Christ (read 2 Corinthians 8–9 and Acts 21: 7-14 in light of Romans 15:25-31 and Galatians 2: 10)! Such material caring for one another created *shalom*. It expressed true love for one another (2 Corinthians 7-8; cf. John 13:34-35). Love of God showed itself in love for the needy brother and sister (cf. 1 John 3:17-18).

5. The Christian church in the next centuries continued to assist in healthcare needs of its own members and those outside the church.

Virtually everyone in the Roman Empire was poor (99 percent); only a few were wealthy. Likewise, the church was composed largely of poor people (1 Corinthians 1:26-28). By A.D. 251, the church in Rome had a massive program of care for widows and the poor. With numerous house churches throughout the city, 1500 people were on the church's support role. Bishop Cornelius was aided by seven deacons, seven more sub-deacons, and ninety-four more working in minor roles to aid the needy (Eusebius, *Ecclesiastical History* 6.43.11). Poor people outside the church community were also helped by the Christians. In light of this model, we ask: how many deacons (or similar caregivers) does your congregation have?

The Roman world treated the poor cruelly, allowing female infants to die with their bodies decaying in open sewers running down the middle of the city streets. Rodney Stark, in his sociological study of early Christianity says, "We've unearthed sewers clogged with the bones of newborn girls." The early Christians "had to live with a trench running down the middle of the road, in which you could find dead bodies decomposing" (Stark, "A Double Take on Early Christianity," *Touchstone* 13/1 [2000]: 44, 47). Christians did not put sewer systems in the cities, but they spoke against infanticide; they cared for each other and those abandoned in a social order blinded to human need.

Though agnostic toward Christianity, Stark is convinced that early Christians made a striking difference in their world: standing for life against death, caring for each other, and valuing women and children, granting them dignity. They lived a counter culture, manifesting God's kingdom values amid a morally bankrupt society. Early Christianity fostered shalom amid horrid healthcare conditions.

Attending to the above five biblical themes and early Christian practices intensifies our concern for the failed U.S. healthcare system. We live in a society where high-tech healthcare innovations are in abundance, often in overlapping availability and competing for the same demographic groups. Yet, skewed distribution of resources, almost endless beginning and end of life expectations, and a for-profit, market-driven system, deprive the needy of healthcare. Is that shalom?

At "Dialogue 1992: The Church Confronts Its Mission in Health and Healing," Dr. Willard Krabill used the image of a "devil's triangle" that exacerbates the healthcare crisis:

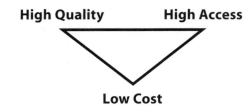

High Quality   **High Access**

Low Cost

Krabill noted that many argue that only by dropping *quality* can *costs* be contained and *access* improved. If we want access for all and/or lower costs, then we must sacrifice quality. Krabill countered the argument, maintaining that all three are possible. To achieve this he called for restraint in high-tech procedures and medical fees, lowering lawyer's fees in malpractice suits (and fewer of them), converting insurance priorities from economic gain to wider coverage policies, breaking the stranglehold of costly pharmaceutical and medical equipment, and conversion from selfish consumerism.

For such a shift to occur, I propose that we view healthcare through new lenses, what I call "God's triangle":

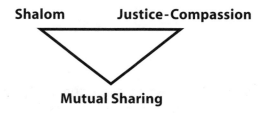

Shalom   **Justice-Compassion**

Mutual Sharing

As we assess the healthcare crisis through these lenses, it becomes an engaging *challenge*. What steps might your church take to wear these glasses?

Lesson 3
The Christian and Anabaptist Legacy in Healthcare

by John D. Roth

"In the name of Jesus Christ of Nazareth, walk!" … Instantly the man's feet and ankles became strong. He jumped to his feet and began to walk. Then he went with them into the temple courts, walking and jumping, and praising God. —Acts 3:6-8

The Early Church: Continuing Christ's Healing Ministry

From the Christian church's beginning, miraculous stories, such as Peter's curing the man outside the temple gates (Acts 3:1-10), make it clear that Jesus's healing ministry would continue through his followers. Accounts of Jesus curing the sick, casting out demons, and restoring life to the dead fill the Gospels. By continuing this ministry of healing, the early church testified to Christ's living presence in their midst. Throughout Acts, "miraculous signs and wonders" of healing frequently accompanied the apostles' call to repentance (Acts 5:12-16; Acts 8:4-7; Acts 9:40-42). Clearly, the ministry of healing—of minds, bodies, spirits, and relationships—was a defining characteristic of early Christianity. Concern for the sick was not unique to early Christians. After all, the Hippocratic Oath originated in Greek culture five centuries before Christ, and the Romans were famous for their curative purges and healing baths. But unlike healthcare in Greco-Roman society, the Christian community's concern for the sick extended beyond the wealthy to include the poor, the orphan, and the stranger. Moreover, the Christian tradition brought an institutional expression to its pastoral concern for the sick that led to a flourishing of hospices, orphanages, and respite centers. Already in 325, the Council of Nicaea commanded that a building dedicated to the care of the sick be constructed in every cathedral town. The hospice of St. Basil at Caesarea in Cappadocia, for example, completed by 370, was renowned for its treatment of the sick and as a place of refuge for travelers and poor people.

Early Christians built similar hospices at Constantinople and Alexandria in Egypt and in cities throughout Syria and Asia Minor.

In Europe, monasteries played a vital role in the care of the sick. Committed to the practice of "hospitality" (from the Latin *hospes*, or host), most monasteries set aside part of their facility as an infirmary for the sick. These early "hospitals" did not so much promise to cure illnesses as to provide a place of relative comfort where the sick could "die a good death" amidst the prayers and ministrations of the pious. Some monastic infirmaries became widely known for the quality of their care. The Hôtel Dieu, for example, founded by the bishop of Paris in the seventh century and still in operation today, was among the most famous of these early hospitals. These more specialized facilities spread rapidly from the eleventh through the fourteenth centuries, often founded as philanthropies of the crusading orders such as the Knights Templars and the Teutonic Knights. During periods of devastating epidemics in Europe—such as the spread of leprosy during the twelfth century or the bubonic plague in the fourteenth century—these church-based hospices provided the afflicted with a small measure of Christian charity and comfort.

Following the Reformation, Catholic monasteries were frequently dissolved in Protestant countries, the secular ruler confiscating their properties. As a consequence, healthcare in Europe increasingly moved from the church's control into the secular hands of the state or private foundations.

The Anabaptist Tradition of Mutual Aid: Communities of Compassion

Born in the tumult of the Reformation, the Anabaptists shared the general Protestant rejection of monasticism. But the monastic ideal of a radical commitment to Christ lived on in

Anabaptist communities, as did the monastic tradition of extending hospitality to the poor and the sick. Although Anabaptists in the sixteenth and seventeenth centuries did not establish formal institutions for healthcare, they were deeply committed to the New Testament principle of "bearing one another's burdens." That commitment inevitably found expression in dealing with physical health and well-being.

In many communities, Anabaptists gained local renown for their skills as midwives, physicians, or healers. In Moravia, for example, the Hutterites were noted for their healing potions, and Hutterite physicians often found employment in the courts of local lords. Mennonites in Switzerland and South Germany frequently found favor with the local population, even during times of severe persecution, as trustworthy midwives, herbalists and veterinarians. The Dutch Mennonites, who enjoyed toleration already in the 1570s, frequently sent their university students to medical school rather than the theological faculties of the state churches; thus, many of their educated pastors in the seventeenth and eighteenth centuries were trained as physicians. One famous Mennonite physician, Govert Bidloo (1649-1713), published an anatomical textbook and served as a professor of medicine in the Dutch town of Leiden.

Why did so many Anabaptists-Mennonites, as a persecuted religious minority, gravitate to the healing arts? Historians have offered several suggestions: unlike farming, medicine was an occupation that did not require heavy investments in land and could easily be "transported" from one region to another; it was a highly valued skill that brought them into favor with the local population even during times of persecution; and it was a pursuit that arose naturally out of their commitment to a life of practical morality and love of neighbor.

The commitment to show Christ's love in daily human relations found more general expression in the Anabaptist-Mennonite tradition of mutual aid—a concern for the needy that went beyond poor relief to include care for the weak, injured, sick, and dying members in their midst. Following the model of the early church, Mennonite congregations appointed deacons whom they charged with the task of addressing the needs of the sick. Mennonite deacons in the urban

congregations of the Netherlands were especially attentive to the medical concerns of poor people in their congregations. One congregation in Amsterdam paid a local surgeon a flat fee to treat anyone in the congregation who was ill. The physician was to provide his own "salve, plasters, gargling fluid, waters and cooling-draughts" while the deacons pledged to provide any necessary medicines from the apothecary. Already in the early seventeenth century, Dutch Mennonites took the lead in establishing hostels (*hofjes*) to provide living quarters and assistance to the chronically ill, the aged, or to members with physical or mental disabilities.

The Dutch Mennonite impulse toward more formal or institutionalized forms of healthcare found even more vigorous expression among related groups of Mennonites who migrated across northeast Germany to Poland and then, in the early nineteenth century, to Russia. In their highly independent colonies in South Russia, healthcare among the Mennonites flourished during the late nineteenth century. Indeed, by the early twentieth century, Russian Mennonites had established several well-equipped hospitals, a mental hospital, several schools for the deaf and blind, a training institute for nurses, and various mutual aid programs that became the forerunners of modern forms of health insurance.

Twentieth-Century Anabaptist-Mennonite Attitudes and Practices

Twentieth-century North American Mennonites have also shown the love of Christ through healing ministries. In the fall of 1908, for example, Mennonites established their first hospital in North America—a sanitarium for the treatment of tubercular patients at La Junta, Colorado, which later expanded into a nurses training college. As North American Mennonites entered vigorously into mission work, a focus on health—including numerous clinics in India, a hospital in Tanzania, and a leprosarium in Paraguay—always accompanied the evangelistic message.

These concerns took on even more public and dramatic expression in the aftermath of World War II. Among the many Mennonite conscientious objectors who chose to enter Civilian Public Service (CPS) camps during the early 1940s, some 1,500 served as attendants in various state institutions for the mentally ill. Deeply troubled by the conditions they witnessed in many facilities, a group of CPSers in Philadelphia began to collect information and concerns, along with constructive ideas for changes, from their fellow workers. Inspired by these reports, *Life* magazine published an exposé of conditions in U.S. mental hospitals (May 1946). Other exposés followed, galvanizing a public outcry that eventually led to the creation of National Mental Health Foundation and a fundamental transformation in American legal and cultural attitudes toward mental illness. The CPS experience in mental health reform also profoundly influenced the Mennonite church. Sponsored by the newly-formed Mennonite Mental Health Services (MMHS), Mennonite-related groups had five mental health centers by the mid-1960s, with another three facilities working in close affiliation with MMHS (now MHS Alliance). "What seems clear," wrote William Klassen, "is that the Mennonites would never have established mental hospitals had they not been spurred on by a corps of dedicated and visionary men who had worked in mental hospitals and become convinced that something could be done for the mentally ill and that the church do something for them."

Since then, the Mennonite commitment to healthcare has continued to flourish. Organizations such as Mennonite Mutual Aid, Mennonite Medical Association, Mennonite Nurses Association, the Mennonite Health Association (1980) and many others have given various visible expressions to the ministry of healing. Increasingly, these organizations have broadened their focus from care for the sick to a more proactive emphasis on wellness—physical, emotional, and spiritual—throughout all stages of life.

As more people are without access to healthcare, as healthcare costs continue to spiral upward, as new technology leads to progressively complex ethical questions, as Mennonite young people increasingly enter health-related professions, and as Mennonites in general become more acculturated into modern society, the call to participate in Christ's ministry of healing remains clear. How Mennonites will continue to answer that call requires careful and thoughtful discernment. But the complexities of the issues ahead should not distract us from the imperative to be ministers of healing.

Lesson 4
Improving Access Locally

by Phyllis J. Miller

When they could not bring him to Jesus because of the crowd, they removed the roof above him; and after having dug through it, they let down the mat on which the paralytic lay. When Jesus saw their faith, he said to the paralytic, " Son, your sins are forgiven." … "But so that you may know that the Son of Man has authority on earth to forgive sins"—he said to the paralytic—"I say to you, stand up, take your mat and go to your home." And he stood up, and immediately took the mat and went out before all of them; so that they were all amazed and glorified God, saying, "We have never seen anything like this!" —Mark 2:1-12

Jesus's ministry included healing people with a variety of illnesses and conditions. Due to its unique emphasis on community, the healing story of the paralyzed man is an especially instructive account as we look at the issue of healthcare access from a local perspective.

Foundational to Anabaptists' beliefs is an emphasis on community and how each person brings unique gifts and talents to be used for service. In this story, the community includes the paralyzed man's friends, who exercise rare creativity in overcoming obstacles to get him to Jesus. What were they thinking that day? Did they realize that their approach was unorthodox? Were they always risk takers? In any case, on that day they steadfastly focused on gaining access to Jesus for their friend. The wider crowd is also part of the community, bearing witness and praising God for the miracle of healing.

As the paralyzed man is surrounded by an activist and witnessing community, our churches too can participate in the healing of persons in our congregations and neighborhoods. Congregational responses to healthcare access are naturally varied and numerous. These responses vary since every congregation has needs and gifts specific to their members and attendees.

Congregational Health Ministries

Some churches have developed Congregational Health Ministries. These efforts sometimes provide direct healthcare access by offering, for example, health screenings. The effort is more indirect in other situations, when, for instance, they furnish needed transportation to healthcare providers. Some congregations hire staff to lead this ministry. Other health ministry programs are entirely volunteer efforts. Examples of these congregational initiatives include the following:

- Health fairs that include health screening and education, targeting areas such as blood pressure, cholesterol, weight and stress management, and administering flu shots.

  ~ *Healthy People 2010* is a set of health objectives intended for all people by the end of the decade. Their web site (www.healthypeople.gov) can assist you in determining a focus for your health fair.

  ~ Mennonite Mutual Aid's downloadable *Stewardship for Life* material covers topics such as exercise, diet, and stress management (www.mma-online.org/education_resources/catalog_descriptions.html).

- Organizing volunteers for respite care provides a much-needed break for family members who attend to loved ones with chronic illness.

- Lending basic durable medical equipment such as walkers, crutches, and canes to members of the congregation is a way of sharing costs and a symbol of Christian stewardship.

- Additional educational events featuring healthcare providers on subjects of interest or need to congregation members. Examples include presentations on drug-to-drug and drug-to-food interactions, managing diabetes, formulating advance directives and assigning healthcare proxies, developments in hospice and palliative care, and ways to lower personal health insurance costs.

Resources for starting Congregational Health Ministries include:

- The Mennonite Nurses Association's web site (www.mna.mennonite.net) has a section on Congregational Health Ministry.

- Nurses' Christian Fellowship offers various resources on parish nursing (www.intervarsity.org/ncf/pn/main.html).

- Mennonite Mutual Aid has developed a resource book on establishing Congregational Health Ministries that is available for purchase at minimal cost (see: www.mma-online.org/production/mmacatalog.nsf/mframe).

Collaborative Projects and Mutual Aid

Besides Congregational Health Ministries, people of faith are locally involved in addressing healthcare access in numerous ways that show commitment and creativity. For example:

- Several physicians banded together to provide healthcare access at limited or no cost for the pastors within their church conference.

- Savings realized by switching to a group health plan were contributed by a congregation to its staff's health savings accounts. Other congregations have special fundraiser events above regular offerings to assure that they can cover health-insurance premiums for their staff.

- One congregation regularly collects mutual aid offerings to assist members with unexpected financial needs, including healthcare access. This money can be used to pay the member's deductibles or medication co-pays, physician fees for surgical procedures, counseling following a traumatic event, and so on.

- Another mutual aid approach to paying for healthcare services is the Mennonite Mutual Aid Sharing Fund. In these situations, the individual or family experiencing hardship, the local congregation, and matching funds from MMA contribute to meeting the healthcare need. Sometimes these funds are used to help pay the premium for a part-time worker who lacks employer-paid insurance or to help cover the premium for a member unable to work while getting treatment for a chronic illness. In other settings, the money might be used to pay large medical expenses that were not covered by or had exceeded the member's health-insurance policy. Specific guidelines for this program can be discussed with your congregational MMA advocate.

- Still another congregation is developing a Mutual Care endowment that will assist in paying for long-term care for older members with insufficient financial resources.

- Some congregations assure health services for their members by partnering with a local hospital and other healthcare providers. The hospital works in collaboration with the congregation's health ministry program and views this partnership as part of its community outreach responsibility, which includes promoting wellness and prevention with the expectation that fewer resources will be needed for treating catastrophic illnesses.

- Several churches collaborated to start a public clinic that cares for individuals in their community who have limited access to other healthcare services. These needed services are provided by a combination of volunteer healthcare personnel and paid staff. The clinic relies on a combination of private donations, grants, and public funding.

- Two excellent resources for congregations interested in exploring collaborative healthcare access projects that reach beyond the congregation:

  ~ Christian Community Health Fellowship (www.cchf.org) "is a national network of Christian health professionals and others concerned about the healthcare needs of impoverished communities in the United

States. We encourage others to live out the gospel through healthcare among the poor." CCHF provides resources and best practices on how communities are responding to these healthcare needs.

~ The Interfaith Health Program of The Carter Center (www.ifpnet.org) is a resource and catalyst to help faith-based communities respond to public health issues in their home communities and beyond.

Awareness-raising Events

For some congregations, the place to start addressing healthcare access is with awareness-raising events.

- Numerous congregations have begun thinking about healthcare access by devoting an entire Sunday to the theme. Scripture readings, hymns, sermon, children's lesson, and Sunday school can focus on healthcare access, providing a starting point for congregational discussion on how you might respond to the issue.

  ~ Materials for a "Healthcare Access Sunday" are available in the "Resources" section of the Anabaptist Center for Healthcare Ethics' web site (www.anabaptistethics.org).

- Alternatively, you may choose to become involved in community-directed awareness events.

  ~ Cover the Uninsured Week, a project of The Robert Wood Johnson Foundation, provides healthcare access event resources for small businesses, healthcare providers, interfaith communities, and college campuses (see the""What You Can Do" section of www.covertheuninsured week.org). This project also provides suggestions for writing letters to the editor and contacting congressional representatives.

As you grapple with healthcare access as a local issue, work to identify tangible needs in your congregation and neighborhood. From these needs, think creatively together about how you might respond as a congregation, group of congregations, or conference. Like the friends of the paralyzed man, be willing to explore options that seem unorthodox and be willing to take risks. Still, because the problems can seem overwhelming, start with something manageable. As you reach those initial goals, you will discover new ways to serve those in your congregation and neighborhood with healthcare access needs.

Lesson 5
Public Policy
by Timothy Stoltzfus Jost

Jesus replied, "Go back and report to John what you hear and see: The blind receive sight, the lame walk, those who have leprosy are cured, the deaf hear, the dead are raised, and the good news is preached to the poor…."
—Matthew 11:4-5 (NIV)

By most measures, the healthcare system of the United States is not good news for the poor. It is not even good news for the comfortable middle class. It is the most expensive system in the world, costing $5,670 per person, more than two-and-a-half times the average expenditure of $2,144 per person for developed countries. Even at this cost, many are excluded: 45 million persons in 2003, and nearly twice that many at some point over a four-year period, lacked health insurance. Over one-third of non-elderly individuals with incomes below the poverty level are uninsured, and lack of health insurance accounts for 18,000 premature deaths each year. Finally, contrary to popular opinion, we do not have the "best" healthcare in the world. Recent studies show that the quality of our healthcare is about average by international standards, good in some things, not so good in others.

There is no perfect healthcare system. Many of us hear Canadian friends complain about their healthcare system (though a 2004 public opinion poll found that only 14 percent of Canadians thought that their healthcare system needed to be "completely rebuilt," compared to 33 percent of U.S. respondents). We likewise hear stories about "rationing" in the British National Health Service. Indeed, most developed countries are struggling with healthcare costs. But on the essential measures of access and cost, all developed countries perform better than the U.S.

Basic Facts about Healthcare in the U.S.

We must understand certain basic facts about healthcare if we are to improve our system. First, the distribution of healthcare costs is radically skewed. In any given year, only 1 percent of the population is responsible for 27 percent of healthcare costs, 5 percent is responsible for over half. By contrast, the least expensive half of the population accounts for 3 percent of healthcare costs in any given year.

This fact has two very important ramifications. First, if health insurance is to be of value for really sick people, it must transfer a considerable share of the cost of healthcare from sick people to healthy people. Second, if our society is to control healthcare costs, we need to figure out how to control the costs of the most expensive 5 percent— controlling the costs of the least expensive 50 percent does almost no good.

A second fact is that healthcare has become too expensive for the poor or near poor. The average employment-related family coverage insurance policy costs over $9,000 per year. For a family of four living at the poverty level, this represents half of all income. Many people living below the poverty level are covered by Medicare, Medicaid, or SCHIP, but many poor people, including working adults without children, are not eligible for these programs. Many poor people must simply go without insurance.

A third fact is that health insurance in the United States is so expensive primarily because we pay high prices for healthcare. We spend less time in the hospital than do residents of most other countries, and we do not see the doctor or use drugs more than people do elsewhere. We just pay higher prices.

A fourth fact is that there is little competition in many healthcare markets, and it is difficult to make competition work in healthcare. Buying healthcare is not like buying breakfast cereal. Next time you are sick, try phoning four local doctors to ask how much it will cost for them to diagnose and treat you. They probably will not be able to tell you (in large part because they will not be able to tell what tests or treatments you will need).

Finally, healthcare is poorly coordinated in the United States. Many people do not have a regular doctor, do not get good preventive care, and change doctors—and thus insurers—every time they change jobs. Americans wait longer to see primary care doctors and are more likely to end up in an emergency room for routine care than are residents of other nations.

How Other Countries Ensure Healthcare Access and Address Costs

What do other countries do to deal with these problems? Most developed countries follow one of two models for paying for healthcare. The older model, established in Germany in the nineteenth century, relies on social insurance (much like our Medicare or Social Security systems). People pay premiums from their wages or pensions, usually calculated as a percentage basis. These premiums are usually administered by nonprofit social insurance funds, which often function much like our Blue Cross/Blue Shield plans used to work. These funds often negotiate with healthcare professionals and providers to set payment rates.

The other model is the national health insurance model, found in the United Kingdom, Scandinavia, Canada, Australia, and elsewhere. Healthcare is paid for by taxes and is available to all at no cost or with a minimal charge. Hospitals are often government owned, but primary care doctors are usually independent business people.

These systems have five key characteristics. First, risk is broadly shared. Such risk sharing is a biblical concept:

> *Our desire is not that others might be relieved while you are hard pressed, but that there might be equality. At the present time your plenty will supply what they need, so that in turn their plenty will supply what you need. Then there will be equality, as it is written: "He who gathered much did not*

have too much, and he who gathered little did not have too little." —2 Corinthians 8:13-15 (NIV)

In Europe this concept of risk sharing is known as "Solidarity." The 5 percent who generate over 50 percent of healthcare costs are helped out by the 50 percent who generate only 3 percent.

Second, wealthier persons care for poorer members of society. To ensure that all are insured, wealthier members of society pay higher taxes or payroll-related premiums. This sense of care also resonates with biblical concerns:

> *Give generously to him and do so without a grudging heart…. There will always be poor people in the land. Therefore I command you to be openhanded toward your brothers and toward the poor and needy in your land.* —Deuteronomy 15: 10-11 (NIV)

Third, because public insurers have market power and are sophisticated buyers, they can hold prices in line. Just as Wal-Mart gets better deals from suppliers than the mom-and-pop grocery store down the street, so do large, national insurance plans. They also often use budgets to control healthcare costs, just as we use budgets to control our household spending. When these are set too low, noticeable rationing may result. However, severe rationing is not a common practice in most developed countries.

Fourth, countries with public insurance pay far less for administrative costs. Unlike private insurers, public insurers do not need to pay for underwriting or marketing, and they do not need to make a profit. Providers also save on administrative costs since they do not deal with multiple private insurers.

Finally, public health insurance in Europe often contributes to better health outcomes by ensuring better coordinated care, longer-term professional/patient relations, and better use of preventive care.

U.S. Proposals

How do the main proposals for expanding healthcare access and controlling healthcare costs in the United States stack up? One idea popular at the moment is to provide tax subsidies to encourage the use of health savings accounts coupled with high-deductible health insurance policies. The idea is that "consumer-driven" healthcare will make individuals more sensitive to costs. This strategy might help the 50 percent of the population with least expensive costs. It will also help employers transfer more of the cost of healthcare to their workers. However, the chronically ill will run through whatever has been contributed to their health savings accounts each year and then have to pay out of their own pockets to cover the gap between those amounts and their deductible. Moreover, most costs of the expensive 5 percent of the population will exceed the deductible and still be covered by insurance. Health savings accounts do little to control these costs. Finally, because individuals have little bargaining power and little ability to get useful price information, "consumer driven" healthcare might result in consumers paying more for care. Empirical evidence to date as to the operation of these plans is discouraging.

Another popular idea is to use tax credits to make health insurance more affordable. This will benefit higher income uninsured people (and over one-quarter of the uninsured have incomes at least 300 percent of the poverty level). Unfortunately, unless credits are set at very high levels, they will not help many poor uninsured families. Current administration proposals would still require families headed by a person aged 45 or older to spend almost $2000 a year to purchase high cost-sharing, low-benefit policies in the nongroup market.

In the end, all other countries have found public insurance programs necessary to assure access for all and to control costs. It is unlikely that the U.S. is so unique that it will find a totally different way.

Lesson 6
What Will We Do? A Call to Action!

by Joseph J. Kotva Jr.

How does God's love abide in anyone who has the world's goods and sees a brother or sister in need and yet refuses help? Little children, let us love, not in word or speech, but in truth and action. —1 John 3:17-18

The Crisis Is Real

Statistics and studies tell part of the story: 45 million uninsured people in the U.S., roughly the population of the West Coast states (including California, Oregon, and Washington) or the combined population of Ohio, Indiana, Michigan, Illinois, and Wisconsin. Studies likewise show that 18,000 premature deaths are attributable annually to lack of insurance, and "1.9-2.2 million Americans (filers plus dependents) experienced medical bankruptcy" in 2001 alone (*Health Affairs*, February 2, 2005). Similarly, a 2003 Kaiser Family Foundation report reveals that 35 percent of the uninsured could not obtain needed care at all.

Economic studies are equally sobering. The Institute of Medicine estimates that the U.S. economy suffers losses between $65 billion and $130 billion per year as a direct result of uninsurance. Even for those with employer-based health insurance, employee health expenses are rising much faster than salaries—for example, from 2000 to 2003, employee contributions to premiums for a family went from $504 to $2,412, and deductibles increased over 50 percent during that same period (ABCNews.com, February 2, 2004). Relatedly, businesses of all sizes report reluctance to hire full-time employees due to expanding healthcare costs (*New York Times*, August 19, 2004). This reluctance is understandable given the projection that "the average annual premium for employer-sponsored family health coverage will surge to $14,545 in 2006" (National Coalition on Healthcare, *Building a Better Healthcare System*, 5).

Statistics and studies point to the healthcare system's severe problems, including runaway costs and millions of people who lack affordable access (see Lesson 1). Such studies fail to communicate the real human pain and loss that is behind those numbers. We gain a deeper sense of these costs by attending to personal stories, such as Gina's (*The Mennonite*, December 7, 2004, 30).

Gina is among the working poor. She has worked in the textile industry since she was 18 and makes enough money to get by, barely. There is enough to pay the rent and buy groceries, clothes, and even an occasional meal at McDonald's. But Gina's income never allows for extras such as cable television and magazine subscriptions, let alone "luxuries" such as health insurance. Gina has a high school education and is active in her church.

Two years ago, at age 48, Gina bought her first home. With interest rates at near historic lows, she discovered that mortgage payments on a modest house were equal to what she was paying in rent. Gina's church was excited for her as they helped her move into the brick house near downtown.

Unfortunately, Gina recently broke her leg walking home from work. It was a freak event: she tripped over nothing in particular, landed awkwardly, breaking her leg. The hospital set the bone, but there were complications over the next several weeks, requiring specialists and two surgeries.

Missed work and lack of health insurance have left Gina in a financial crisis. She is behind on her mortgage, and the hospital is badgering her to pay her mountain of medical debts. Gina is filled with anxiety. She fears losing her house. She cannot pay the hospital bill, even if they were willing to spread it over ten years. Her church wants to help, but they cannot generate that much money. A lawyer acquaintance suggests that Gina consider bankruptcy—something that she views as a humiliating sign of personal failure.

Gina's situation is not unique. Due to increasingly high co-payments and uncovered treatments, lost work, and the outright lack of health insurance, millions of hard-working, lower and middle income individuals and families are one health crisis away from financial ruin. But Gina at least received medical treatment, unlike Rick.

Rick is 22 and works at a popular coffee shop. He struggles with bipolar disorder, usually experiencing months of stability, but then slowly slipping into mania or falling dramatically into depression. He has no health insurance since the coffee shop does not provide coverage. Because he has a "pre-existing condition," Rick cannot purchase individual insurance, even if he could afford it. He has looked unsuccessfully for employment that includes health insurance.

During recent bipolar episodes, Rick received no treatment because he lacks insurance. During these times, Rick's family and friends do what they can to be supportive, but they are angry that Rick is shut out of the healthcare system. They do not understand the healthcare system's indifference as they helplessly watch their creative son and friend become "someone else."

There are millions of "Ginas" and "Ricks" out there. Their stories are the substance behind the statistics and studies. Our healthcare system is in crisis and real people pay the price. What will we do about it?

A Call to Action

Faced with this crisis, inaction is not an option. The New Testament is clear that Christian love tangibly responds to the needs of others. First John 3:17-18 challenges us to love in truth and action by meeting the needs of our sisters and brothers in the church. The story of the good Samaritan involves administering a type of healthcare for a stricken stranger (Luke 10:29-37). In his collection for the poor in Jerusalem, Paul calls the church in Corinth to uncoerced generosity, which he sees as a test of their love (2 Corinthians 8:7-8). And in the scene where the Son of man separates people as sheep from goats, attending to the sick is among the basic actions that reveal our hearts and upon which we are judged (Matthew 25:31-46).

Christian love responds concretely to the needs of others. And, as Willard Swartley (Lesson 2) and John Roth (Lesson 3) illustrate, healing and healthcare are prominent, tangible expressions of love throughout the New Testament and church history. Faced with the healthcare crisis, inaction is not an option for our Anabaptist Christian communities.

Recent history suggests that we might prefer inaction. Proposals to reform healthcare, including the plan associated with Hillary Clinton, abounded in the political ferment of the early 1990s. During this national focus on healthcare, some Anabaptist-related groups passed healthcare resolutions. The Church of the Brethren Annual Conference (1989) and the Church of the Brethren General Board (1992), the General Conference Mennonite Church U.S. (July 1992), and the Mennonite Church General Assembly (July 1993) passed resolutions calling for both government action and congregational commitment to address growing problems in healthcare.

Regrettably, most Anabaptist-related communities have not maintained the energy that went into those thoughtful documents. With the rest of the nation, many of them wearied of the often contentious healthcare debates. Since the mid-1990s, most have given little attention to the healthcare crisis.

Halfway into the 2000s, the situation continues to worsen and is again a topic of national conversation. So too, Anabaptist communities, with many other faith communities, are calling for changes in healthcare. We thus have a renewed opportunity to love in truth and action by attending to needed changes in healthcare. Since the issues are complex and the political climate is contentious, such attention will require sustained commitment to both local (see Lesson 3) and national (see Lesson 4) efforts.

What Will We Do?

To respond to the healthcare crisis, we must evaluate the needs around us and the gifts, skills, and interests present within our communities. Congregations with numerous physicians and nurses will likely respond differently than congregations made up of educators, factory workers, and local politicians. Most congregations, individually or collectively, can creatively respond to the problems in healthcare. Such responses are of several types: reduced expectations, wellness and prevention, local access initiatives, and political action.

One factor driving healthcare costs is our **ever-increasing expectations** of what medical technology can deliver, especially at the beginning and end of life. As expressions of Christian stewardship and testimonies to God's care, we can become better educated about these issues and use advance directives (living wills and proxies) to state our limited expectations of that technology. We can likewise find ways to engage the faith community in decision making that is willing to limit the use of medical technologies in assisted reproduction and the artificial prolongation of life.

Other responses will focus on **wellness and prevention**. While the precise healthcare costs are unclear, the prevalence of substance abuse, smoking, and obesity (plus related issues such as poor diet and inadequate exercise) exact an enormous toll in disease and death. These are complex realities involving both individual choices and strong cultural and social forces. It is therefore best to avoid focusing on individual blame. Instead, operating from the conviction that life and health are God's gifts to which we respond in grateful stewardship, our congregations can offer regular blood pressure screening, diabetes testing, exercise and nutrition classes, and so on.

Since its earliest days, the Christian church engaged in **local healthcare initiatives**, including hospices, orphanages, and respite centers (see Lesson 3). Options today for such initiatives are as wide as our imagination and commitment. For example, Anabaptist-related communities in the West have partnered with church agencies to sponsor a dental van, community education events on nutrition, and a public-health advocate. Perhaps your congregation(s) can start, volunteer at, or fund-raise for a local free clinic. Or, perhaps you can help fill out the pharmaceutical vouchers that many drug companies provide for fixed and low income individuals. (See Lesson 4 for more examples.)

The level of local initiatives is also where we can fruitfully engage employers and healthcare providers about their role in ensuring healthcare access. Most Anabaptist employers furnish their employees with generous wages and benefits, and most healthcare providers and administrators offer compassionate care. It is also true that most non-elderly in the U.S. receive health insurance through their own or a family member's employer ("Uninsured Workers in America," The Henry J. Kaiser Family Foundation, July 2004). It is equally true that healthcare providers are the front line of healthcare access. Given these realities, we should encourage Anabaptist employers to explore means to provide access to health insurance coverage for employees and their dependents. We should likewise encourage healthcare providers to consider how some profit can be redirected to improve healthcare access for the poor. Perhaps your congregation can creatively partner with local employers and healthcare providers to better enable them to provide coverage and care.

Other congregations will best respond to the healthcare crisis through **political action**. All other developed countries do better than the U.S. in providing access to healthcare and controlling the relevant costs. In every case, government plays an essential role in achieving these objectives. So too, the magnitude and complexity of the problem in the U.S. means that approaching a real "solution" will require significant federal government coordination and expenditure. (Lesson 5 overviews how other countries handle healthcare and what we might say to our elected officials.)

The rationale for speaking to government on behalf of such reform includes the role of health and healing in the New Testament as signs of God's reign (Matthew 9:35; Luke 7:18-23), our concern for justice (Deuteronomy 16:20; Micah 6:8; Matthew 23:23) and love of neighbor (Matthew 22:39; Galatians 5:14), Jesus's call for fundamental social change (Luke 4:16-21), and our belief that Christ is finally Lord over all persons and powers (Acts 10:36; Philippians 2:9-11; Colossians 1:16-20). There are, of course, different ways to speak to government. We can communicate directly through phone and letter-writing campaigns or visiting officials in their DC or regional offices. Some will prefer more symbolic communication, such as the 10,000 person "Bridging the Gap for Healthcare" walk across the Golden Gate Bridge on June 19, 2004.

However we respond, the crisis in healthcare presents us with both an obligation and an opportunity to "love … in truth and action" (1 John 3:18).

STUDY GUIDE

With Reproducible Handouts

By Dale Shenk

Teacher Orientation

by Dale Shenk

The following lesson plans are designed to guide small group conversations about the six essays that form this study. Before beginning the study, please read the following paragraphs.

A. **Introduction—Each lesson begins with a set of instructions for the teacher to follow in the days before the lesson is to be taught. These instructions provide background information that will better enable you to teach the lesson well.**

B. **Components—Each lesson contains several basic components that appear in slightly different forms and sequences. Being familiar with them will help you understand and anticipate how the class will respond from session to session.**

   a) Context—At some point in each lesson remind students of the earlier lessons and call attention to the way that this specific lesson fits into the overall scheme of the series.

   b) Focus—The first portion of the session invites class participants to consider the lesson's theme by examining their own experiences and perspectives. This conversation sets the stage for the more direct learning that follows. It also provides an opportunity to develop a pattern of broad sharing within the class.

   c) Bible Study—Each lesson includes references to Scripture. In some cases, such as Lessons 2 and 3, they are the heart of the lesson; in others the biblical teachings are more peripheral. In each case, you will be invited to consider the biblical framework surrounding the particular teaching.

   d) Information Gathering—Each lesson also has some instruction about the current healthcare system, in many cases providing information and perspectives that will be new to most class members. It is important to take time for this somewhat academic portion of the conversation that may at times require a lecture style presentation.

   e) Commitment—Each lesson will end with a call to commitment. Class participants can respond to this call with an internal response of confession or commitment to learning. Toward the end of this series, class participants may respond by committing themselves to some public action regarding the healthcare situation.

C. **Assumptions—Besides the explicit components listed above there are some more implicit assumptions in these instructions:**

   a) The lesson plans developed here are loosely based on the Praxis model of education as articulated by Thomas Groome. This approach, used by publishing bodies in the Mennonite church for several years, will be familiar to teachers who have used other denominational materials. Lessons in this format begin with some conversation that is based on the personal experience and perspectives of the participants. The conversation then moves to the text, which in this case are twofold: the Scriptures and healthcare system information. The session closes with a response or commitment to action that develops from the lesson.

b) The student body of the class may change from session to session. With that in mind each lesson is presented to make sense to a student who was not in attendance at the previous one. Regular students will see and understand the obvious connections. But other than a short introduction, you will not need to do an in-depth review of each session to bring all of the students up to speed.

c) Some class participants will not have a copy of the study guide; others will not read the materials carefully before the class; still others will only have time for a superficial reading. The handout is intended to alleviate this situation somewhat. In addition to the handout, you as teacher will need to have a comprehensive understanding of the essay so that you are able to bring the insights of the author into the class at appropriate times in the conversation.

d) Each lesson offers more material than you will have time for in a single 45-50 minute session; thus, you will need to focus on that portion of the lesson's material that the class will likely find most hopeful.

This is a United States conversation. While this issue is certainly relevant worldwide, the specific information, material, and perspectives assume that the persons in this conversation are aware of and participants in the U.S. healthcare system.

The Current Situation
Teacher Preparation

Be sure that you know the story of how your class came to be taught in its specific setting. If you are the healthcare advocate for your congregation, you may already be able to share most of this story. If you have been asked by others to teach this material, talk with them further about the overall purpose of this class.

Review the six lessons in the series, and be able to summarize each one in a sentence or two. This summary will help the class understand the study's overall scope and trajectory and will remind them where you as a class have been and where you are going. It may also be useful to give a brief introduction to each writer. Short author bios are provided at the end of this guide.

Look at the questions that the author, Karl Shelly, asks. Jot down answers that members of your class might give to these questions. Consider whether the class will be able to understand and agree or disagree with Shelly. How will you prepare for that part of the discussion?

Read each of the Scripture passages and look at the context of each text. Shelly quotes only short sections, especially in the opening paragraph. What can you say about the chapters from which these references come? Additionally, it may be helpful to look further at a Bible commentary on the Mark 5 story that Shelly uses at the end of the lesson.

The Session

A. Context—Ask the class the following questions:

a) What do you expect from this class? (Why are you here?) Get responses from as many people as possible. If the class is large, divide them into groups of 3-4 and have them answer the question in those smaller clusters.

b) Why is our congregation offering this course? Open this question up to the whole group. If they are uncertain of the answer, provide one from your earlier conversations with congregational leadership.

c) Briefly outline the six sessions. You may want to use a variation of the following:

   i. Session 1 invites us to consider the "health" of healthcare in the United States.

   ii. Session 2 helps us examine the basic biblical teachings on healthcare.

   iii. Session 3 reviews the history of Christian commitment to healing ministries.

   iv. Session 4 helps us explore ways that we can respond to local healthcare needs.

   v. Session 5 is an assessment of the U.S.'s healthcare system as compared to other national systems.

       vi. Session 6 challenges us to commit ourselves to action regarding the healthcare situation.

B. Focus—Introduce the specific theme of today's session with some of the following questions:

  a) Explore the personal experience of the class with the healthcare system.

    i. When have you needed healthcare? What was the experience like?

    ii. Have you ever not been able to get needed healthcare? What happened? Or, what would have happened if you had not been able to get needed care?

    iii. What did it cost immediately? Were there long-term costs?

  b) Assess the current healthcare system in the United States:

    i. What are its strengths? Weaknesses? Look at the opening comments on the handout summarizing the strengths and weaknesses.

    ii. What has your experience been with the system?

    iii. Are you insured? How? Or, when did it end?

    iv. Do you know people who are not insured? Why do they not have coverage?

C. Bible Teaching—Look at the three Scripture passages that are noted in the opening paragraph. These suggest the theological context for the whole study. Invite participants to read silently the section from which this quote comes. Use the following questions to go deeper in these passages:

  a) Ezekiel 34:16—Expand the study by using 34:2-5 and 34:15-16: The context of this passage is the exile of the people of Israel. The people are judged for not taking care of the sick. Does this sound like the healthcare situation in the U.S.? Is that fair?

  b) John 10:10—How are abundant life and healthcare connected? Note that earlier in the passage there is a comparison between the Good Shepherd and the stranger.

  c) Matthew 25:40—This is among the most challenging New Testament passages. Look at 25:35-36 for a more specific list of what is expected. Are the members of the class or the congregation as a whole doing these things?

D. Read Mark 5:24b-34. Note the points that Shelly makes about this passage:

  a) The healthcare system was not helpful for the woman in the story.

  b) Jesus saw her as a daughter.

c) Jesus delays his trip in order to minister to her.

d) Jesus heals her.

e) *Also worth noting:* Some scholars suggest that this woman's act of touching Jesus was in violation of the Jewish holiness codes of the day. An extreme punishment for this may have been death. If this is true, Jesus's act is even more gracious.

E. Information Gathering—Read Shelly's four questions that are listed on the handout. Ask the class which question they would like to consider. Or go through the list one at a time. Use the following pattern for each one:

a) Read the question.

b) Read the answers.

c) Is this surprising?

d) Are these statistics true of the people that you know? Why? Why not?

F. Commitment—End the session with a time of prayer. The length of this period of prayer will depend on how the session has progressed. Plan on including in the prayer the elements of thanksgiving, confession, and openness to the Spirit's leading. Lead the prayer yourself or use the following phrases to guide a time of silence.

a) Thanksgiving—We are thankful that God has given us the ability and resources to care for ourselves and others when we are sick. We are especially thankful for the healthcare workers who are called to this field.

b) Confession—We confess that we participate in a healthcare system that does not provide care for everyone who needs it.

c) Openness—We want to be open to the Holy Spirit's leading. May we grow in our understanding and our faithfulness through the remainder of these lessons.

G. Evaluation—Spend a few minutes after the session assessing the time together. Use the following questions to help guide future conversations:

a) Were the attendance patterns and participation healthy? Do you anticipate this changing throughout the series?

b) What comments and questions need to be addressed at some future point? Were there suggestions that need further planning or that need to be passed on to other groups in the congregation?

The Current U.S. Healthcare Situation

The United States at its best has as good medical care as you'll get anywhere in the world. It really is superb.—Herbert Pardes, MD, President and CEO of New York Presbyterian Healthcare Network (2000)

The United States has a disintegrating, profit-ridden healthcare non-system. … The stories of real people confronting their healthcare problems show how cruel our system has become.—Dr. John P. Geyman, Professor Emeritus of Family Medicine, University of Washington (2002)

Is our healthcare system "superb" or "cruel"?

- **Strengths:** World leading advancements in diagnostic technology, high-tech treatments, and pharmaceuticals

- **Weaknesses:** Millions of citizens unable to access not only the latest advances but basic healthcare services; poorer healthcare outcomes for the population as a whole (compared to other countries) despite leading the world in per capita healthcare spending

What might the Bible say about healthcare access? (NRSV)

- **Ezekiel 34:15-16**—I myself will be the shepherd of my sheep, and I will make them lie down, says the Lord God. I will seek the lost, and I will bring back the strayed, and I will bind up the injured, and I will strengthen the weak, but the fat and the strong I will destroy. I will feed them with justice.

- **John 10:10-11**—The thief comes only to steal and kill and destroy. I came that they may have life, and have it abundantly. I am the good shepherd. The good shepherd lays down his life for the sheep.

- **Matthew 25:40**—And the king will answer them, "Truly I tell you, just as you did it to one of the least of these who are members of my family, you did it to me."

- **Mark 5:34**—He said to her, "Daughter, your faith has made you well; go in peace, and be healed of your disease."

How do most people access healthcare in the United States?

- Nearly two-thirds of Americans under the age of 65 are insured through their own or a family member's employer.

- The percentage of Americans with employer-sponsored coverage has been declining every year since 2000.

Who are the people without health insurance?

- Forty-five million Americans—more than one in six of the nonelderly population—are uninsured.

- The number of uninsured has grown by over 1 million persons each of the past four years.

- Four out of five of the uninsured are in working families. Two-thirds of the uninsured had household incomes under $50,000.

- In 2003, 33 percent of Hispanics and 20 percent of African-Americans were uninsured.

What are the consequences of being uninsured?

- Eighteen thousand people a year, under age 65, die prematurely as a consequence of being uninsured.

- For many, being uninsured means having poorer health and no regular source of care, including basics such as blood pressure checks, cholesterol readings, and various cancer screenings.

- "The uninsured receive less preventive care, are diagnosed at more advanced disease stages, and once diagnosed, tend to receive less therapeutic care (drugs and surgical interventions)" (Kaiser Commission on Medicaid and the Uninsured, "Sicker and Poorer: The Consequences of Being Uninsured" [February 2003]).

- Thirty-five percent of the uninsured report being unable to obtain needed care at all (see lesson 6).

- "1.9-2.2 million Americans (filers plus dependents) experienced medical bankruptcy" in 2001 alone (Health Affairs [February 2, 2005]) (see lesson 6).

- Low(er) wage workers report frequent problems paying their medical bills and forgoing needed healthcare (The Commonwealth Fund, Task Force on the Future of Health Insurance [October 2004] (see lesson 6).

How does the U.S. healthcare system compare internationally?

- Spends more per capita on healthcare than any other country.

- Has state-of-the-art medicine

- Latest technology is accessible to those able to pay and those with adequate insurance

- Is the only industrialized developed country that does not assure coverage for everyone.

- Consistently places below 20th in criteria such as life expectancy, infant mortality, and immunization rates.

The Bible and Christian Convictions
Teacher Preparation

Again be prepared to outline the series for the class. Review the previous session's materials to find ways to make connections between that conversation and this one. This review will also help class participants to anticipate the upcoming lessons.

The biblical teaching in this session is deep and complex. You will need to select the themes that make sense for your class. Consider which points will be new or challenging, hence, most productive. The specific practical questions that are addressed in items 4 and 5 of the handout may need the least attention.

Prepare by looking up all the Bible passages from each section. Swartley carefully defines *shalom* and *justice*. Review the verses that he refers to so that you understand the reasoning process. You may also find a verse and insight to which you want to give special attention.

Each person in the class will need access to a Bible. In some settings participants will bring their own, or you may want to collect enough for the class.

Depending on class size, it may be easier to divide the class into small groups, giving each group one "key point" from the handout. After reading the handout and the corresponding Scripture verses (and, if available, the lesson materials) on their assigned topic they should be ready to present the main insights and teaching of their "key point" to the rest of the class. This presentation would include their group's answers to the question that follows each section.

Swartley suggests two additional exercises that may be instructive for your class:

- A deep sense of koinonia permeated the early church's life and experience of mutual care. Perhaps someone in the class can do a study of koinonia in the New Testament.

- For fuller understanding of mutual aid practice in early Christianity, someone in class might read Swartley's article, "Mutual Aid Based in Jesus and Early Christianity," in *Building Communities of Compassion,* eds. Donald B. Kraybill and Willard M. Swartley (Scottdale, Pa.: Herald Press, 1998), 21-39.

The Session

A. **Focus—Begin the class with a brief overview of this series. Include a two or three sentence summary of the conversation from the previous session. Then move to the following questions:**

   a) What do you think the Bible has to say about healthcare?

   b) If you were going to preach a sermon on healthcare, what passage(s) would you use?

   c) Have you ever thought about your health insurance decision as biblical?

B. **Alternative Focus**—If the class has already carefully read the lesson material, you might want to ask for general responses:

   a) Was the use of these passages to teach about healthcare surprising?

   b) Did the teaching make sense? Especially on *justice* and *shalom*?

   c) With which topics do we need to spend the most time?

C. **Bible Teaching**—Swartley provides several basic and helpful questions. Use the handout summaries to guide the discussion. Pay attention to time so that you address the questions that you believe are the most important for the class. Following are additional questions to help you to expand the discussion:

   a) Shalom

      i. Does the class understand the difference between this definition of shalom and the more typical understanding that it means "peace"?

      ii. Is it possible for some of the community to be experiencing shalom while another part does not?

   b) Justice

      i. Should justice be linked with the *rights of* the poor or *compassion for* the poor?

      ii. Is the class comfortable with the idea that God's *wrath* is directed against those who do not care for the poor?

   c) Inclusive Healing

      i. Are there contemporary equivalents of the groups of persons listed here?

      ii. What is our witness to the powers on this topic? (Ephesians 3:9-10)

   d) Sharing Resources

      i. Is sharing in your congregation formal and organized? Or does it happen informally when there is a need?

      ii. Does your congregation share more readily when the needs are local or farther away? Emotional needs or physical needs?

   e) Deacons—

      i. Who in your congregation has this kind of caring as a part of their job description?

      ii. Could this be added to the gift-discernment process?

D. Information Gathering—Review the triangles that Swartley describes:

a) Ask the class to place a dot within the "Devil's Triangle" that represents the current balance between the competing points of healthcare. In a small class this could be done on a board; in a large class you might want individuals to place a dot on their handouts. Then they can share their responses briefly with the person sitting beside them. Be sure to allow some time to compare the answers as a class. Discuss whether the current balance between the points of the triangle is ideal or not.

b) Review Krabill's argument that all three are possible. These items are listed on the handout.

c) Examine "God's Triangle." Are the same dynamics present here? How would you position the current healthcare system within this triangle? How does your congregational healthcare approach embody these three dynamics? Will mutual sharing result in justice? Or shalom? How? Do these triangle elements almost demand each other? Does Krabill's response to the "Devil's Triangle" line up with this new triangle from Swartley?

E. Commitment

a) Take time to invite responses to this lesson. A likely result of this biblical teaching is that many class participants learned something new. Ask them to name those new insights as a way of confirming and strengthening the learning.

b) Encourage those with copies of the study guide to prepare for the next session by reading John Roth's article. As they read it, they might want to ask, "Has the church been faithful to the biblical principles (such as justice and shalom) covered in today's session?"

F. Evaluation—Spend a few minutes after the session assessing the time together. Use the following questions to help guide future conversations:

a) Were the attendance patterns and participation healthy? Do you anticipate this changing throughout the series?

b) What comments and questions need to be addressed at some future point?

c) Were there suggestions that need further planning or that need to be passed on to other groups in the congregation?

Biblical and Theological Convictions

Christians who hold to a love-ethic for all people have a greater moral obligation and should be more motivated than are non-Christians to care deeply about healthcare access for all.

Key Points of a Biblical and Theological Basis of Passion for a Better Healthcare System

1. Scripture identifies *shalom* (Genesis 26:6; 37:14; 43:27; Exodus 18:7; 1 Samuel 10: 4; 17:18, 22; 25:5; 30:21; Jeremiah 15:5 for shalom of Jerusalem; 38:4) as God's will and gift for people with many dimensions of meaning: wholeness, well-being, peace, salvation, and even justice.

Is access to healthcare God's "will and gift"?

2. The Old Testament strongly emphasizes justice. The biblical understanding of justice often occurs in parallel to righteousness (Psalm 72:1-2; Proverbs 2: 9; Isaiah 5:7b; 32:16; 33:5-6) and shalom/peace (Isaiah 32-16-17; 59:8). Justice means caring for the poor, widows, and orphans (Psalm 12:5; 72:4, 12-14; 146: 6b-9) that is motivated by compassion and mercy.

How does this understanding compare with common notions of justice in our culture?

3. Jesus modeled healthcare inclusion of the poor and marginalized. Approximately a third of those Jesus healed were women. Some that Jesus healed were ritually defiled, unclean. Another third were socially ostracized, lepers, Gentiles, and "sinners." When we consider the social, economic, and political profile of the people Jesus healed and hear his teaching (such as Matthew 25:31-40), we learn a basic, important lesson about healthcare access: exclusionary policies in healthcare are wrong.

Do you agree or disagree with this statement?

4. Sharing material resources is a basic teaching and practice of the New Testament church. After Pentecost the early church initially had all things in common (Acts 2:42-45; 4:32-37). Another model of sharing involved collecting money from wealthier Jewish-Gentile Christian churches for the poorer Jewish Christians in Jerusalem (2 Corinthians 8-9; Romans 15:15-27).

What practices of mutual aid for healthcare do you have in your congregation?

5. The Christian church in the next centuries continued to assist in healthcare needs of its own members and those outside the church. By A.D. 251 the church in Rome had a massive program of care for widows and the poor. With numerous house churches throughout the city, 1,500 people were on the church's support role. Bishop Cornelius was aided by seven deacons, seven more sub-deacons, and ninety-four more working in minor roles to aid the needy (Eusebius, *Ecclesiastical History* 6.43.11).

How many deacons (or similar care-givers) does your congregation have?

Devil's Triangle

At a Healthcare Conference ("Dialogue 1992"), Dr. Willard Krabill used the image of the "devil's triangle" exacerbating the healthcare crisis, with the competing goals of:

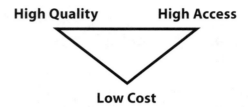

High Quality   **High Access**

Low Cost

Krabill noted that many argue that only by dropping *quality* can *costs* be contained and *access* improved. If we want access for all and/or lower costs, then we must sacrifice quality.

Krabill countered by maintaining that all three are possible. To achieve this he called for:

- Restraint in high-tech procedures and medical fees

- Lowering lawyer's fees in malpractice suits (and fewer of them)

- Converting insurance priorities from economic gain to wider coverage policies

- Breaking the stranglehold of high pharmaceutical and costly medical equipment

- Conversion from selfish consumerism.

God's Triangle

For such a shift to occur, and in light of the five key biblical and theological points, Swartley proposes that we conceptualize our desired healthcare system through "God's triangle":

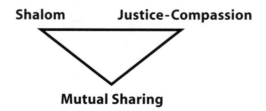

Shalom   **Justice-Compassion**

Mutual Sharing

What steps might your church take to see through God's triangle?

The Christian and Anabaptist Legacy in Healthcare
Teacher Preparation

Again be prepared to outline the series for the class. Review the last session's materials to find ways to make connections between that conversation and this one. This review will also help class participants to anticipate the upcoming lessons.

This essay is heavily weighted toward factual content. Much of this material will be new for most class participants, at least in the details. It is therefore necessary that you spend additional time familiarizing yourself with the lesson's content. One option is to make a timeline of the materials. If you ask the class to make a timeline, making your own in advance will allow you to illustrate the activity and prepare you to recognize gaps and confusion in their work. The handout is set up to help you with this activity. List all of the Christian church's efforts at health and healing in chronological order. Attach dates to each effort so that you can appreciate the consistency of the church's healthcare activity across history.

Another way to approach the factual content is to provide reading time during the lesson. This would create some common ground for the class members.

The Session

A. Focus

a) How is the church involved in healthcare in your community?

b) What hospitals, clinics, or other agencies are rooted in a Christian response to physical needs?

B. Information Gathering—There are three suggestions for this section of the lesson. If you have time and enough copies of the guide, you may want to begin with some silent reading. Shape this time by having participants look at the timeline on the handout. This starting point provides them with clues about what to look for in their reading.

If you have more limited time, consider one of the following options. If the class tends to depend on you to familiarize them with the material, use option (a). If the class has demonstrated a commitment to reading the material ahead of time, use option (b).

a) Timeline—Work as a class to develop a timeline of all of the ways that John Roth describes the church as responding to health needs in history. This activity is simplified by working through the lesson materials one paragraph at a time. If the class is large, assign sections of the lesson to smaller groups. Next put the work up on a white board in the front of the room. Several healthcare activities are repeated in different forms throughout the list. Allow those repetitions as the timeline develops.

b) Reflect on the timeline (or on the reading they did if you begin with this item).

    i. Are there repeated activities?

    ii. Are there noticeable gaps?

    iii. Are there new developments?

    iv. How has the church responded to major events in history, such as a war or health crisis?

Discussion Points—Roth offers three excellent questions, listed on the handout, which focus on the relationship between miracles and medicine, the interplay of the church and state, and the specific locus of responsibility for healthcare needs. Besides those somewhat theoretical questions, below are questions that look at specific historical situations. Choose which type of questions will be most helpful for your class.

1. If miracles were such a significant part of the early church response, should these be emphasized more today?

2. Imagine together what the "hospitality" (hospital wing) of a monastery would have been like without the healthcare resources that we have today.

3. Does the class understand how the Protestant Reformation decreased the healthcare resources in Europe?

4. Explore the reasons that are given for the presence of so many Mennonites in the healing arts. Are these reasons still valid?

5. Review the role of deacon as mentioned in this lesson. Remind the class of the reference to deacon in the last session.

6. Review the story of the development of mental health institutions in the late twentieth century. There may be people in your congregation with personal experience in this story.

C. **Bible Teaching**—Roth uses the early chapters of Acts as a beginning point in his description of a Christian response to health needs. Some of these same teachings were noted in previous lessons. Several biblical passages are also referenced on the handout. If you have time, look at these texts and consider how they inform our responses to current healthcare needs. Additional relevant biblical texts include:

a) Acts 2:42-47; 4:32-37; 6:1-6—How is the community formed so that it is prepared to respond to needs?

b) Acts 3:6-8; 5:12-16; 8:4-8; 9:40-42—What is the role of these miraculous healings in the preaching of the gospel? Do you see parallels between these stories of healing and those done by Jesus in the Gospels?

c) Mark 6:7-13 and James 5:14-15—What role did anointing with oil play in these texts? Does your congregation practice anointing with oil?

Additional Note: The handout includes quotes from various Anabaptist statements that directly or indirectly bear on this lesson's theme. One way to review these quotes would be to explore how they grow out of Scripture. Several quotes show this connection explicitly.

D. Commitment—This lesson offers many reasons to celebrate the presence of the church in history. This same reflection also serves as a challenge to us.

Offer a prayer of thanksgiving for the church and its ministry of healthcare over the centuries. This prayer should also challenge the class to continue the church's witness in health and healing.

E. Evaluation—Spend a few minutes after the session assessing the time together. Use the following questions to help guide future conversations:

a) Were the attendance patterns and participation healthy? Do you anticipate this changing throughout the series?

b) What comments and questions need to be addressed at some future point?

c) Were there suggestions that need further planning or that need to be passed on to other groups in the congregation?

Christian and Anabaptist Legacy in Healthcare

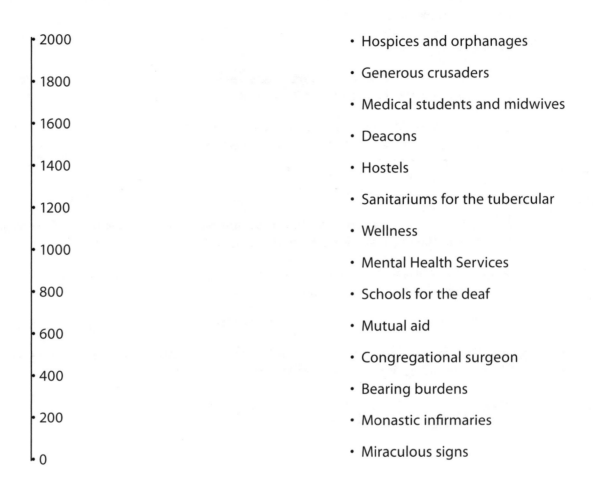

2000	• Hospices and orphanages
1800	• Generous crusaders
	• Medical students and midwives
1600	• Deacons
1400	• Hostels
1200	• Sanitariums for the tubercular
	• Wellness
1000	• Mental Health Services
800	• Schools for the deaf
600	• Mutual aid
	• Congregational surgeon
400	• Bearing burdens
200	• Monastic infirmaries
0	• Miraculous signs

Discussion Questions

1. What have we gained/lost as a result of the transformation from the New Testament emphasis on the dramatic and miraculous presence of the Spirit to our present focus on the promises of modern science?

2. Should Christians lobby for government legislation that would demand higher standards of care for the mentally disabled or focus more on creating alternative church-related mental health facilities that would operate according to Christian principles?

3. Who should bear the responsibility for the well-being of those people outside the church who don't have access to decent healthcare?

Excerpts from Anabaptist-Mennonite Confessions and Statements

The Dordrecht Confession (1632), Article 9

That they should also see diligently to it, particularly each among his own over whom he has the oversight, that all places be well provided with deacons (to look after and care for the poor), who may receive the contributions and alms, in order to dispense them faithfully and with all propriety to the poor and needy saints (Acts 6:3-6).

And that also honorable aged widows should be chosen and ordained deaconesses, that they with the deacons may visit, comfort, and care for, the poor, feeble, sick, sorrowing and needy, as also the widows and orphans, and assist in attending to other wants and necessities of the church to the best of their ability (1 Timothy 5:9; Romans 16:1; James 1:27).

Confession of Faith in a Mennonite Perspective 1995 (excerpts from Article 10)

… The church is called to witness to the reign of Christ by embodying Jesus's way in its own life and patterning itself after the reign of God. Thus it shows the world a sample of life under the lordship of Christ. By its life, the church is to be a city on a hill, a light to the nations, (Matthew 5:13-16; Isaiah 42:6) testifying to the power of the resurrection by a way of life different from the societies around it.

The church is also to give witness by proclaiming the reign of God in word and deed…. The church is called to be a channel of God's healing, which may include anointing with oil (Mark 6:13; James 5:14-15).

Mennonite Brethren Confession of Faith (excerpts from Articles 14 and 15)

We believe that all human life belongs to God. Each person is created in the image of God and ought to be celebrated and nurtured. Because God is creator, the author and giver of life, we oppose all actions and attitudes which devalue human life. The unborn, disabled, poor, aging and dying are particularly vulnerable to such injustices. Christ calls the people of all nations to care for the defenseless.

Christians do not claim any of their possessions as their own, but manage all their resources, including money, time, abilities and influence, in generous ways that give glory to God. They do not despise the poor but practice mutual aid within the church and share what they have with others in need. God's people seek to embrace a lifestyle of simplicity and contentment.

Statement on Healthcare in the United States (1989) Church of the Brethren Annual Conference

Our Judeo-Christian heritage has taught us that God's holy purpose includes everyone, that every person is of worth. As God's people, we are to be concerned for the health of all people, and to nurture health for one another. In the past, the church has accepted the responsibility of caring for others; today the church is called to a new level of involvement. As God's people on earth, the church is called to work for high quality, comprehensive healthcare for all.

Improving Access Locally
Teacher Preparation

Again be prepared to outline the series for the class. Review the last session's materials to find ways to make connections between that conversation and this one. This review will also help class participants to anticipate the upcoming lessons.

This lesson's primary focus is on the healthcare issues that face your congregation locally. It will benefit your class if you are prepared with specific information about your local situation. We suggest the following methods for gathering additional information:

- Visit people in the congregation that work in healthcare-related fields. The doctors and nurses of the congregation will have practical knowledge and experience to offer in this situation. They will also bring balance to the brainstorming that is planned for later in the session.

- If you do not have a person in your congregation who can provide this background, seek out someone in the community. Check with other congregations.

- Have a similar conversation with people in the social services or welfare field. They will be able to describe your community's specific situation, and will know both what resources are available and are needed. They will also have some idea about relevant costs.

- Go to the public library and look for census information that describes the healthcare needs of your town or city. You may need a librarian's assistance in finding this information, but it will be a valuable resource for your class conversation.

- Visit each of the web sites that are suggested in the lesson. Identify one or two that are especially relevant or helpful for your congregation.

The Session

A. Focus

a) Review the study so far. We began by discussing problems with the current healthcare system. The past two sessions have focused on the biblical and historical responses to healthcare needs. The next three lessons begin to invite the class members and the congregation to commit themselves to improving healthcare access in the community and nation.

b) Reflect on this learning by asking some of the following questions:

   i.   What concerns you the most about healthcare access?

   ii. What are the new things that you have learned so far?

   iii. Are some truths about healthcare still difficult to accept?

   iv. Are you sensing a need to do something specific?

B. **Bible Teaching**—Let members of the group take turns reading the study passage from Mark 2:1-12. You may also want to read the story from Matthew 9:2-8 and Luke 5:18-26, or Mark's account in several translations. This text can also be acted out as a drama. The physical acts of helping a friend on a stretcher can deepen appreciation for the story.

Use the following questions to consider how the story reflects an act of community:

a) What elements of community do you see in the text?

b) How might this community have been formed?

c) What are the possible motivations of the friends?

d) What do you think led up to this event?

e) What happened next?

f) What might this story teach us about responding to healthcare access?

C. **Information Gathering**—The lesson describes several ways that congregations are already responding to healthcare access issues. Take time to list those actions. The handout lists some of these actions and also includes web sites that offer more specific descriptions. For those with copies of the guide, ask them to skim the lesson to gather additional ideas. To help clarify the steps toward commitment, develop a list of possibilities on a board that is visible to the class. Here are some likely responses:

a) Organizing or supporting health screening events

b) Coordinating of transportation to healthcare services

c) Providing information on health

d) Volunteering for respite care

e) Coordinating durable equipment loans

f) Hosting educational events

g) Encouraging physician groups to provide care

h) Opening a clinic

i) Partnering with a hospital

j) Organizing fundraisers to provide benefits

k) Receiving mutual aid offerings

l) Collaborating with Mennonite Mutual Aid's "sharing fund" (which provides matching funds for many congregational programs related to health and wellness)

m) Providing mutual financial care for older members, perhaps through an endowment

n) Planning a Health Access Sunday

D. Commitment

a) Think concretely together about healthcare access needs in your community.

   i. What are the access needs of your particular congregation? Of your church neighborhood or community?

   ii. If you do not already know those needs, how might you sensitively identify unmet healthcare needs?

   iii. How might your congregation respond to those identified needs?

   iv. With whom might you work in your neighborhood and community in responding to the identified healthcare access needs?

   v. How might you work with other congregations or your conference to respond to access needs?

   vi. What is the next concrete step that your group needs to take to begin addressing healthcare access in your setting?

b) Close with prayer that remembers the specific concerns that were shared in the session's first part and the beginning plans that the class made in the last part. Seek God's leading in determining and motivating the class and the congregation's next steps in addressing healthcare access.

E. Evaluation—Spend a few minutes after the session assessing the time together. Use the following questions to help guide future conversations:

a) Were the attendance patterns and participation healthy? Do you anticipate this changing throughout the series?

b) What comments and questions need to be addressed at some future point?

c) Were there suggestions that need further planning or that need to be passed on to other groups in the congregation?

Improving Access Locally

A Community's Commitment to Healthcare Access

When he returned to Capernaum after some days, it was reported that he was at home. So many gathered around that there was no longer room for them, not even in front of the door; and he was speaking the word to them.

Then some people came, bringing to him a paralyzed man, carried by four of them. And when they could not bring him to Jesus because of the crowd, they removed the roof above him; and after having dug through it, they let down the mat on which the paralytic lay.

When Jesus saw their faith, he said to the paralytic, "Son, your sins are forgiven." Now some of the scribes were sitting there, questioning in their hearts, "Why does this fellow speak in this way? It is blasphemy! Who can forgive sins but God alone?"

At once Jesus perceived in his spirit that they were discussing these questions among themselves; and he said to them, "Why do you raise such questions in your hearts? Which is easier, to say to the paralytic, 'Your sins are forgiven,' or to say, 'Stand up and take your mat and walk'?"

But so that you may know that the Son of Man has authority on earth to forgive sins—he said to the paralytic—"I say to you, stand up, take your mat and go to your home."

And he stood up, and immediately took the mat and went out before all of them; so that they were all amazed and glorified God, saying, "We have never seen anything like this!"—Mark 2:1-12

Discussion Questions

1. What elements of community do you see in the text?

2. How might this community have been formed?

3. What are the possible motivations of the friends?

4. What do you think led up to this event?

5. What happened next?

6. What might this story teach us about responding to healthcare access?

Possibilities

Some congregations establish health ministries that provide health screenings and educational events. Others furnish needed transportation to healthcare providers or to have a church space where wheelchairs, walkers, and crutches are stored until needed. Still others develop creative financial mechanisms to meet their members' uncovered healthcare expenses.

1. What are the access needs of your particular congregation? Of your church neighborhood or community?

2. If you do not already know those needs, how might you sensitively identify unmet healthcare needs?

3. How might your congregation respond to those identified needs?

4. With whom might you work in your neighborhood and community in responding to the identified healthcare access needs?

5. How might you work with other congregations or your conference to respond to access needs?

6. What is the next concrete step that your group needs to take to begin addressing healthcare access in your setting?

Resources

For more information on how your congregation might respond to healthcare access needs, here are some beginning resources:

- Cover the Uninsured Week, a project of The Robert Wood Johnson Foundation: www.covertheuninsuredweek.org

- Mennonite Nurses Association, including a section on parish nursing: www.mna.mennonite.net

- Nurses' Christian Fellowship provides parish nursing resources: www.intervarsity.org/ncf/pn/main.html

- Mennonite Mutual Aid provides resources on wellness and Congregational Health Ministry: www.mma-online.org/education_resources/catalog_descriptions.html and www.mma-online.org/production/mmacatalog.nsf/mframe

- Interfaith Health Program of The Carter Center: www.ihpnet.org

- Healthy People 2010 includes health objectives for all persons by the end of the decade: www.healthypeople.gov

- Christian Community Health Fellowship provides resources and best practices for responding to the healthcare needs of impoverished communities: www.cchf.org

- Anabaptist Center for Healthcare Ethics, including resources for a Healthcare Access Awareness Sunday: www.anabaptistethics.org

Public Policy

Teacher Preparation

Again be prepared to outline the series for the class. Review the last session's materials to find ways to make connections between that conversation and this one. This review will also help class participants to anticipate the final stages of the study.

This essay includes somewhat technical information regarding the healthcare system. Read the material carefully so that you understand the statistical points that Timothy Stoltzfus Jost is making. Look at the graphs carefully. Be sure that you understand the issues. In addition, you may want to call on one of your healthcare "experts" from Lesson 4 to help you understand the issues presented in this essay. You may want to compare the points made in this essay with the "Devil's Triangle" and "God's Triangle" from Lesson 2.

The Bible passages that are used here are part of much larger stories. Spend some time with the Old Testament passages in Deuteronomy 15 and Leviticus 25. Chapter 4 of *Rich Christians in an Age of Hunger* by Ron Sider offers valuable perspectives on these passages. Chapter 5 in *The Upside-Down Kingdom* by Donald B. Kraybill is also helpful.

Spend some time thinking about what political action might look like for your congregation. Is this a politically active congregation? Do some church members participate in political organizations, local boards, counsels, etc.? Are there congregation members with experience in coordinating letter writing campaigns or visiting with legislators?

The Session

A. **Context—Review the series themes. Remind class participants that the previous session examined ways we can respond in the local context. Check to see if some details from the past week need further conversation. For example, if there was strong interest in doing a specific local project, ask if planning is going well.**

B. **Focus**

   a) What are class perceptions of the U.S. healthcare system? Have these changed during the study?

   b) Test the critique of our healthcare system as outlined in the lesson. The handout includes a summary of the problems and two illustrative graphs.

   i. Read through "Healthcare Problems in the U.S." one point at a time.

   ii. Ask if this is new information and if it fits with what they have learned in previous sessions.

   iii. Ask if the participants agree or disagree with each point. (You will not get complete agreement on every point. Allow diverse perspectives to be shared.)

iv. Pay attention to the explanations that people give for agreement or disagreement. It may be helpful to highlight the primary resources to which class members appeal.

C. Information Gathering—

a) Using the chart and points from the handout, work to understand how other countries organize healthcare.

 i. Do the participants understand the column headings?

 ii. How are we like these countries in other ways? Make some comparisons between the U.S. and these countries, particularly the high levels of industrialization, education, culture, and faith history.

b) Respond to the handout section "What do other countries do differently?"

 i. Are these worthwhile goals? Why or why not? What do they have in common with the biblical principles from Lesson 2?

 ii. Which points do the participants find most powerful?

 iii. Is there something that they would like to see in a healthcare system that is not on this list?

D. Bible Teaching—Read the verses that are given on the handout and in the lesson and look at the backgrounds of these texts.

a) 2 Corinthians 8:13-15—The setting for this text (discussed in Lesson 2) is Paul's request to support poorer Jewish Christians in Jerusalem. It also may be noted that wealthier Corinthians had been challenged in 1 Corinthians 11 to overcome class distinctions during communion. Invite participants to tell stories of times when they experienced need or plenty and the ways that the broader community became a means of support or a mechanism of sharing.

b) Deuteronomy 15:10-11—You may want to look at the broader context (Deuteronomy 15:1-18) here as well. The sabbatical year required that people trust God to provide and was a means of ensuring economic justice: debts are forgiven and slaves are set free and given resources to establish themselves. Sometimes the phrase "there will always be poor in the land" is used as an excuse to limit giving. Note that this text uses that phrase to insist upon generosity. How does this Scripture passage meet the accusation that poor people simply need to work harder?

c) Compare the biblical principles you have identified with the list of characteristics of other national healthcare plans. How are they similar? Different?

    i. Shared risk

    ii. Wealthier care for the poorer

    iii. National plans hold down costs

    iv. Administration is less expensive

E. Commitments

a) Political Action

    i. What actions are the participants willing to make in response to this lesson?

    ii. How might this information be shared with others?

    iii. How can public policy be changed?

    iv. What is the next concrete step that your group needs to take to carry out those actions?

b) Prayer—close with prayer for the government. This is a time to specify in your prayer the kinds of actions to which God is calling officials.

F. Evaluation—Spend a few minutes after the session assessing the time together. Use the following questions to help guide future conversations:

a) Were the attendance patterns and participation healthy? Do you anticipate this changing throughout the series?

b) What comments and questions need to be addressed at some future point?

c) Were there suggestions that need further planning or that need to be passed on to other groups in the congregation?

The Policy Context

Healthcare Problems in the U.S.

"It is the most expensive system in the world, costing $5,267 per person, two and a half times the average expenditure of $2,144 per person for developed countries. Even at this cost, many are excluded: 45 million persons." —Timothy Stoltzfus Jost

- Most money is used on a small percentage of the population

- Poor and lower income people cannot afford care on their own

- Our prices are higher than other developed countries for all medical goods and services

- Little existing competition and difficult to make competition work in healthcare

Poor coordination

1996 Health Care Expenditures by Percentage of Total U.S. Population

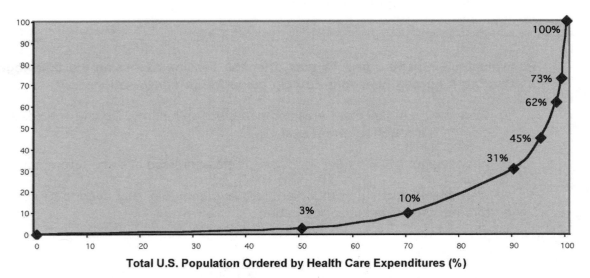

Total U.S. Population Ordered by Health Care Expenditures (%)

Source: Berk and Monheit, "Concentration of Health Expenditures," Health Affairs 20(2) 9 (2001)

This chart shows that in our current healthcare system, most of the costs come from a very small percentage of people. Look at a few examples from the chart. Only 50 percent of the population spends 3 percent of all of the money that is spent in healthcare; 5 percent of the population spends 55 percent.

Let's look at this same information as if there are 100 people and they need to spend a total of $100 on healthcare. Fifty people will need only a total of $3 of care. Another 40 people will need only a total of $28 of care. The last 10 people will need the remaining $69 of care.

The International Context

Country	Universal Coverage	Total expenditure on health % of GDP (2003)	Total expenditure on health, per capita (US$ 2003)	Life Expectancy at birth (2001) males/females	% of population who rates care received from doctor excellent
United States	No	14.6	5267	74.4 79.8	61%
Germany	Yes	10.9	2817	75.6 81.3	
Canada	Yes	9.6	2931	77.1 82.1	68%
United Kingdom	Yes	7.7	2160	75.7 80.4	64%

Source: OECD data, Commonwealth Fund International Comparative Data

What do other countries do differently?

- First, risk is broadly shared. The 5 percent who generate over 50 percent of healthcare costs are helped out by the 50 percent who generate only 3 percent.

- Second, wealthier people care for poorer. Wealthier members of society pay higher taxes or payroll-related premiums to make sure that all are insured.

- Third, public insurers in other countries have enough market power that they can hold prices in line. They also use budgets to control healthcare costs, just as we use budgets to control our household spending.

- Fourth, countries with public insurance pay far less for administrative costs. Unlike private insurers, public insurers do not need to pay for underwriting or marketing, and they do not need to make a profit.

Bible Teaching

I do not mean that there should be relief for others and pressure on you, but it is a question of a fair balance between your present abundance and their need, so that their abundance may be for your need, in order that there may be a fair balance. As it is written, "The one who had much did not have too much, and the one who had little did not have too little." —2 Corinthians 8:13-15

When have you experienced need or plenty and in what ways did the broader community become a means of support or a mechanism of sharing?

Give liberally and be ungrudging when you do so, for on this account the Lord your God will bless you in all your work and in all that you undertake. Since there will never cease to be some in need on the earth, I therefore command you, "Open your hand to the poor and needy neighbor in your land." —Deuteronomy 15:10-11

How does this scripture meet the accusation that poor people simply need to work harder?

Discussion Questions

1. Do you understand the difficulties in our current system?

2. Do you understand the strengths in some of the other options?

3. Do you understand the biblical teachings on this issue?

What Will We Do? A Call to Action!
Teacher Preparation

This is the study's final session. Hopefully momentum is building so that the class is ready to begin, or already has begun, responding to the healthcare crisis discussed in this series. Prepare carefully so that learning from the series is summarized carefully and future plans are clearly defined.

Review the five previous lessons in order to summarize the series for the class. This review will be especially helpful for class members who have not attended each session. Your notes and reflections from the evaluation at the end of each session will likely show which points need to be emphasized.

Plan some way to follow up on the Information Gathering portion of the session. These ideas will be relevant to the leaders in your congregation who initiated this study.

The Session

A. Focus

a) Review the five previous lessons. Keep the review brief; at this point you can assume that most class members have participated enough to understand the study's basic flow. A basic overview is also on the handout.

  i. Lesson 1—The U.S. healthcare system suffers from runaway costs, millions of people without proper access to healthcare, and poor performance in key health outcomes such as life expectancy and infant mortality.

  ii. Lesson 2—The biblical ideals of shalom and justice, Jesus's healing ministry to the poor and marginalized, the New Testament and early church's example of sharing material resources, and innovative work in healthcare teach us to work for healthcare that is accessible to all.

  iii. Lesson 3—The Christian church has acted throughout history to provide healthcare for the sick and the poor. Anabaptists in particular gained renown for their attention to healing, mutual aid, the development of hospitals and training institutes for nursing, and their pivotal role in transforming U.S. mental hospitals.

  iv. Lesson 4—We can learn from what other churches and people of faith are already doing as we meet the call to use our unique gifts to address creatively the local healthcare access needs of both fellow church members and our neighbors.

  v. Lesson 5—There are alternatives to the way the U.S. provides healthcare. We can learn from how other developed countries coordinate healthcare, all of whom use public insurance programs to do better than the U.S. in controlling costs and providing access.

b) Ask participants to share what they have learned.

  i. What has been new?

  ii. What is still hard to believe?

  iii. What have we done as a congregation?

  iv. What do people want to do?

B. **Bible Teaching—There are two ways to work with the Scriptures in this lesson. One focuses on the passages that this final essay uses to summarize the study, two of which are used in earlier lessons. The other looks back at all of the passages used in the series. This will take more time, but it will also deepen the learning through review. You might choose a combination approach by reviewing especially the passages or ideas that are repeated.**

  a) Texts from Lesson 6

    i. First John 3:17-18—Whose needs are to be met, according to this passage?

    ii. Luke 10:29-37—Whose needs are to be met?

    iii. Second Corinthians 8:7-8—How are needs met?

    iv. Matthew 25:31-46—What are the consequences of not meeting needs?

  b) Overview of biblical texts

    i. Lesson 1

      1. Ezekiel 34:16—Exile in Babylon is seen as punishment for ignoring the poor

      2. John 10:10—Jesus gives abundant life

      3. Matthew 25:40—Judgment on those who do not care for the sick

      4. Mark 5:24-34—Jesus healed an outcast

    ii. Lesson 2

      1. Shalom—(Overview)

      2. Justice—Psalms (Overview)

      3. Jesus as a model of healing—(Overview)

      4. Acts 2 and 4—Mutual care in the congregation

iii. Lesson 3

   1. Acts 2 and 4—(Repeated)

   2. Acts 3:6-8 and others—Miracles

   3. Mark 6:13 and James 5:14-15—anointing with oil

iv. Lesson 4

   1. Mark 2:1-12—Community involved in achieving healthcare access

v. Lesson 5

   1. Second Corinthians 8—Community generosity

   2. Deuteronomy 15—Caring for the poor

C. **Information Gathering—Joseph Kotva suggests four ways to respond to the U.S. healthcare situation. These are noted on the handout. To engage those four suggestions, choose one of the following:**

a) Divide the class randomly into four groups. Assign a different suggestion to each group. Have them work for the rest of the time on a specific and practical way that this congregation could act on their assigned suggestion.

Practical Suggestions

   i. Keep the groups to 3-5 persons. If you have a large class, assign some suggestions to more than one group.

   ii. You might divide into groups based on their interest.

   iii. Each group should appoint a recorder so that group's work is not lost when the session ends.

b) Choose to emphasize one suggestion and work as a group on a plan of action in that area. The result of this option may have significant authority and power in the congregation since it originates from a larger group.

c) If your class is already working at a response to Lessons 4 and 5, use this time as a work session to continue the process.

d) Kotva spends additional time helping us understand how political action can be useful. Since political action may be a new option in some Anabaptist congregations, spending additional time on this lesson material may prove worthwhile.

D. **Commitment**—Gather the written work of the groups. If there is time, invite sharing from each group. Close with prayer for those who need healthcare, those who provide it, and all Christians as we are called to respond to human need.

E. **Summary**—Complete the series by meeting with the congregation's leadership to communicate what transpired during the series, especially the last session. Be sure to share with leadership the written reports from Lesson 6.

Please also share the written reports with the producers of this Guide, the Anabaptist Center for Healthcare Ethics (ACHE). Send those reports to:

ACHE at AMBS

3003 Benham Ave.

Elkhart IN 46517-1999

Alternately, e-mail the reports to the ACHE's director, Joseph Kotva, at: jkotva@ambs.edu

What Will We Do? A Call to Action!

- Lesson 1—The U.S. healthcare system suffers from runaway costs, millions of people without proper access to healthcare, and poor performance in key health outcomes.

- Lesson 2—The biblical ideals of shalom and justice, Jesus's healing ministry, and the example of the early church teaches us to work for healthcare that is accessible to all.

- Lesson 3—As Anabaptist Christians, we have a rich history of mutual aid, caring for the sick and the poor, and transformative work in mental healthcare.

- Lesson 4—We can learn from what others are already doing as we meet the call to use our unique gifts to address creatively the local healthcare access needs of both fellow church members and our neighbors.

- Lesson 5—We can learn from how other developed countries coordinate healthcare, all of whom use public insurance programs to do better than the U.S. in controlling costs and providing access.

- Lesson 6—A Call to Action

Biblical Call to Action

- 1 John 3:17-18 challenges us to love in truth and action by meeting the needs of our sisters and brothers in the church.

- The story of the Good Samaritan involves administering a type of healthcare for a stricken stranger (Luke 10:29-37).

- In his collection for the poor in Jerusalem, Paul calls the church in Corinth to uncoerced generosity, which Paul sees as a test of their love (2 Corinthians 8:7-8).

- In the scene where the Son of Man separates people as sheep from goats, attending to the sick is among the basic actions that reveal our hearts and upon which we are judged (Matthew 25:31-46).

Necessary Actions

Adjusted Expectations

As expressions of Christian stewardship and testimonies to God's care, we can become better educated about the issues of medical technology at the beginning and end of life and use advance directives (living wills and proxies) to state our limited expectations. We can likewise establish mechanisms for engaging the faith community in decision making that is willing to limit the use of medical technologies in assisted reproduction and the artificial prolongation of life.

Wellness and Prevention

While the precise healthcare costs are unclear, the prevalence of substance abuse, smoking, and obesity (plus related issues such as poor diet and inadequate exercise) exact an enormous toll in disease and death. These are complex realities involving both individual choices and strong cultural and social forces. It is therefore best to avoid focusing on individual blame. Instead, operating from the conviction that life and health are God's gifts to which we respond in grateful stewardship, our congregations can offer regular blood pressure screenings, diabetes testing, exercise and nutrition classes, and so on.

Local Initiatives

Since its earliest days, the Christian church engaged in local healthcare initiatives, including hospices, orphanages, and respite centers. Options today for such initiatives are as wide as our imagination and commitment. For example, Anabaptist-related communities in the West have partnered with church agencies to sponsor a dental van, community education events on nutrition, and a public-health advocate. Perhaps your congregation(s) can start, volunteer at, or raise funds for a local free clinic. Or, perhaps you can help fill out the pharmaceutical vouchers that many drug companies provide for fixed and low-income individuals. This level of local initiatives is also where we can fruitfully engage Christian employers and healthcare providers about their ongoing role in ensuring healthcare access.

Political Action

The rationale for speaking to government on behalf of healthcare reform includes the role of health and healing in the New Testament as signs of God's reign (Matthew 9: 35; Luke 7:18-23), our concern for justice (Deuteronomy 16:20; Micah 6:8; Matthew 23: 23) and love of neighbor (Matthew 22:39; Galatians 5:14), Jesus's call for fundamental social change (Luke 4:16-21), and our belief that Christ is finally Lord over all people and powers (Acts 10:36; Philippians 2:9-11; Colossians 1:16-20). There are, of course, different ways to speak to government. We can communicate directly through phone and letter writing campaigns or visiting officials in their DC or regional offices. Some will prefer more symbolic communication, such as the 10,000 person "Bridging the Gap for Healthcare" walk across the Golden Gate Bridge on June 19, 2004.

Contributors

Timothy Stoltzfus Jost, JD holds the Robert L. Willett Family Professorship of Law at the Washington and Lee University School of Law. He is a coauthor of a casebook, Health Law (West Group Publishing, 2000), used widely throughout the United States in teaching health law, and is the author of numerous articles and books on health law and policy, including *Disentitlement? The Threats Facing Our Public Health-Care Programs and a Rights-Based Response* (Oxford University Press, 2003).

Joseph J. Kotva Jr. pastored in eastern Pennsylvania for ten years before becoming director of the Anabaptist Center for Healthcare Ethics (ACHE). He has written numerous books and articles on themes in Christian ethics, particularly in clergy ethics, virtue ethics, and medical ethics. He is married to Carol and they have two boys, Joseph and Matthew. He especially enjoys playing trumpet in their family band.

Phyllis J. Miller is a nurse and healthcare consultant, and works with organizations and healthcare managers in leadership development and performance management. She also teaches in the health services management track of the MBA program for DeVry University and is the current president of the Mennonite Nurses Association. She is a graduate of Eastern Mennonite University and the University of Maryland, and is a member of Washington Community Fellowship of Washington, DC.

John D. Roth is professor of history at Goshen College where he also serves as director of the Mennonite Historical Library and editor of *The Mennonite Quarterly Review*. He is the author of *Choosing Against War: A Christian View* (Good Books, 2002) and *Beliefs: Mennonite Faith and Practice* (Herald Press, 2005). He and his wife Ruth are the parents of four teenage children and are active members at Berkey Avenue Mennonite Fellowship in Goshen, Indiana.

Karl S. Shelly is co-pastor at Assembly Mennonite Church (Goshen, Indiana) and adjunct professor in the Goshen College Peace, Justice and Conflict Studies department. He previously worked on U.S. healthcare policy in the Mennonite Central Committee Washington Office.

Dale Shenk was a pastor in Pennsylvania and Indiana for ten years. For the past 12 years he has been on the Bible and Church History faculty at Bethany Christian High School. During this time he also served as moderator of Indiana Michigan Conference and as overseer of several congregations in northern Indiana. From 2003–2004 he worked for Eastern Mennonite University and Lancaster Mennonite Conference to develop pastoral training materials. He has written Herald Press Sunday school materials for adult and youth. Dale lives in Goshen, Indiana, with his wife Trish and their three children.

Willard Swartley is professor emeritus of New Testament at the Associated Mennonite Biblical Seminary, Elkhart, Indiana. From 1989–2002 he was the New Testament editor for the *Believers Church Bible Commentary* series; his publications include *Slavery, Sabbath, War and Women: Case Issues in Biblical Interpretation* (Herald Press, 1983), and *Israel's Scripture Traditions and the Synoptic Gospels: Story Shaping Story* (Hendrickson, 1994). He and his wife, Mary, enjoy visiting their two children and six grandchildren.

Notes:

Notes: